T0311417

An Analysis of

Thomas Paine's

Common Sense

Ian Jackson

Published by Macat International Ltd
24:13 Coda Centre, 189 Munster Road, London SW6 6AW.

Distributed exclusively by Routledge
2 Park Square, Milton Park, Abingdon, Oxon OX14 4RN
711 Third Avenue, New York, NY 10017, USA

Routledge is an imprint of the Taylor & Francis Group, an informa business

www.macat.com
info@macat.com

Cataloguing in Publication Data
A catalogue record for this book is available from the British Library.
Library of Congress Cataloguing-in-Publication Data is available upon request.
Cover illustration: Etienne Gilfillan

ISBN 978-1-912303-41-0 (hardback)
ISBN 978-1-912128-67-9 (paperback)
ISBN 978-1-912282-29-6 (e-book)

Notice
The information in this book is designed to orientate readers of the work under analysis,
to elucidate and contextualise its key ideas and themes, and to aid in the development
of critical thinking skills. It is not meant to be used, nor should it be used, as a
substitute for original thinking or in place of original writing or research. References and
notes are provided for informational purposes and their presence does not constitute
endorsement of the information or opinions therein. This book is presented solely for
educational purposes. It is sold on the understanding that the publisher is not engaged
to provide any scholarly advice. The publisher has made every effort to ensure that
this book is accurate and up-to-date, but makes no warranties or representations with
regard to the completeness or reliability of the information it contains. The information
and the opinions provided herein are not guaranteed or warranted to produce particular
results and may not be suitable for students of every ability. The publisher shall not be
liable for any loss, damage or disruption arising from any errors or omissions, or from
the use of this book, including, but not limited to, special, incidental, consequential or
other damages caused, or alleged to have been caused, directly or indirectly, by the
information contained within.

CONTENTS

WAYS IN TO THE TEXT
Who Was Thomas Paine?   9
What Does *Common Sense* Say?   10
Why Does *Common Sense* Matter?   11

SECTION 1: INFLUENCES
Module 1: The Author and the Historical Context   14
Module 2: Academic Context   18
Module 3: The Problem   22
Module 4: The Author's Contribution   26

SECTION 2: IDEAS
Module 5: Main Ideas   31
Module 6: Secondary Ideas   35
Module 7: Achievement   39
Module 8: Place in the Author's Work   43

SECTION 3: IMPACT
Module 9: The First Responses   47
Module 10: The Evolving Debate   51
Module 11: Impact and Influence Today   55
Module 12: Where Next?   58

Glossary of Terms   62
People Mentioned in the Text   68
Works Cited   72

THE MACAT LIBRARY

The Macat Library is a series of unique academic explorations of seminal works in the humanities and social sciences – books and papers that have had a significant and widely recognised impact on their disciplines. It has been created to serve as much more than just a summary of what lies between the covers of a great book. It illuminates and explores the influences on, ideas of, and impact of that book. Our goal is to offer a learning resource that encourages critical thinking and fosters a better, deeper understanding of important ideas.

Each publication is divided into three Sections: Influences, Ideas, and Impact. Each Section has four Modules. These explore every important facet of the work, and the responses to it.

This Section-Module structure makes a Macat Library book easy to use, but it has another important feature. Because each Macat book is written to the same format, it is possible (and encouraged!) to cross-reference multiple Macat books along the same lines of inquiry or research. This allows the reader to open up interesting interdisciplinary pathways.

To further aid your reading, lists of glossary terms and people mentioned are included at the end of this book (these are indicated by an asterisk [*] throughout) – as well as a list of works cited.

Macat has worked with the University of Cambridge to identify the elements of critical thinking and understand the ways in which six different skills combine to enable effective thinking.
Three allow us to fully understand a problem; three more give us the tools to solve it. Together, these six skills make up the **PACIER** model of critical thinking. They are:

ANALYSIS – understanding how an argument is built
EVALUATION – exploring the strengths and weaknesses of an argument
INTERPRETATION – understanding issues of meaning

CREATIVE THINKING – coming up with new ideas and fresh connections
PROBLEM-SOLVING – producing strong solutions
REASONING – creating strong arguments

To find out more, visit **WWW.MACAT.COM.**

CRITICAL THINKING AND *COMMON SENSE*

Primary critical thinking skill: REASONING
Secondary critical thinking skill: CREATIVE THINKING

Thomas Paine's 1776 *Common Sense* has secured an unshakeable place as one of history's most explosive and revolutionary books. A slim pamphlet published at the beginning of the American Revolution, it was so widely read that it remains the all-time best selling book in US history.

An impassioned argument for American independence and for democratic government, *Common Sense* can claim to have helped change the face of the world more than almost any other book. But Paine's pamphlet is also a masterclass in critical thinking, demonstrating how the reasoned construction of arguments can be reinforced by literary skill and passion. Paine is perhaps more famous as a stylist than as a constructor of arguments, but *Common Sense* marries the best elements of good reasoning to its polemic. Moving systematically from the origins of government, through a criticism of monarchy, and on to the possibilities for future democratic government in an independent America, Paine neatly lays out a series of persuasive reasons to fight for independence and a new form of government. Indeed, as the pamphlet's title suggested, to do so was nothing more than 'common sense.'

ABOUT THE AUTHOR OF THE ORIGINAL WORK

Born in Britain in 1737, **Thomas Paine** had a humble, religious upbringing and very little formal education. The course of his life turned in 1774, when he met the great American statesman Benjamin Franklin in London. With Franklin's help, Paine emigrated to the American colonies, where his political writings such as *Common Sense* contributed to the discontent that resulted in the American Revolution. Paine maintained his stubborn commitment to morality and social justice until his death in 1809 in New Rochelle, New York at the age of 72.

ABOUT THE AUTHOR OF THE ANALYSIS

Ian Jackson is a PhD student in the Politics, Philosophy and Religion department at Lancaster University. He is interested in the role new media plays in the dissemination of ideas.

ABOUT MACAT

GREAT WORKS FOR CRITICAL THINKING

Macat is focused on making the ideas of the world's great thinkers accessible and comprehensible to everybody, everywhere, in ways that promote the development of enhanced critical thinking skills.

It works with leading academics from the world's top universities to produce new analyses that focus on the ideas and the impact of the most influential works ever written across a wide variety of academic disciplines. Each of the works that sit at the heart of its growing library is an enduring example of great thinking. But by setting them in context – and looking at the influences that shaped their authors, as well as the responses they provoked – Macat encourages readers to look at these classics and game-changers with fresh eyes. Readers learn to think, engage and challenge their ideas, rather than simply accepting them.

'Macat offers an amazing first-of-its-kind tool for interdisciplinary learning and research. Its focus on works that transformed their disciplines and its rigorous approach, drawing on the world's leading experts and educational institutions, opens up a world-class education to anyone.'

Andreas Schleicher
Director for Education and Skills, Organisation for Economic Co-operation and Development

'Macat is taking on some of the major challenges in university education … They have drawn together a strong team of active academics who are producing teaching materials that are novel in the breadth of their approach.'

Prof Lord Broers,
former Vice-Chancellor of the University of Cambridge

'The Macat vision is exceptionally exciting. It focuses upon new modes of learning which analyse and explain seminal texts which have profoundly influenced world thinking and so social and economic development. It promotes the kind of critical thinking which is essential for any society and economy. This is the learning of the future.'

Rt Hon Charles Clarke, former UK Secretary of State for Education

'The Macat analyses provide immediate access to the critical conversation surrounding the books that have shaped their respective discipline, which will make them an invaluable resource to all of those, students and teachers, working in the field.'

Professor William Tronzo, University of California at San Diego

WAYS IN TO THE TEXT

KEY POINTS

- Though born in England in 1737, Thomas Paine is best remembered for writing pamphlets that inspired Americans to revolt against Great Britain.

- *Common Sense* called for American independence and explained how to achieve it.

- Paine's pamphlet made political ideas accessible and sold in huge numbers. It directly influenced the outcome of the American Revolution*—the military conflict that led to the independence of 13 of Great Britain's North American colonies and the formation of the United States of America.

Who Was Thomas Paine?

Thomas Paine was born in England in 1737. His father belonged to the Quakers,* a denomination of Christianity that opposes war and violence. Though few received an education at this time, and Paine's family was not rich, he attended a grammar school*—what we would today call a "secondary" or "high" school—until he was 13. There he received a basic education in Latin, Greek, mathematics, and the Scriptures.

Paine's early life was not particularly successful. Neither of his marriages lasted, and the businesses he started failed. In 1772, while working for the Customs and Excise Office inspecting imported goods, Paine wrote his first political work, *The Case of the Officers of Excise*, in which he argued for better working conditions and pay. He was dismissed from this post early in 1774.

In September 1774, Paine was introduced to Benjamin Franklin,* an inventor, author, and political agitator who would become one of the Founding Fathers of the United States of America. Franklin was impressed with Paine, and he not only advised him to move to North America, but also gave him a letter of recommendation.

When Paine arrived in Philadelphia, the political situation in the American colonies was quite volatile. The Seven Years War,* fought between Great Britain and France over conflicting trade interests, had ended 11 years earlier. While Great Britain had won, it was heavily in debt and wanted the colonies to help cover the war's cost. Paine, like many Americans, was outraged that Britain would tax the colonies to help pay for the war while refusing them representation in Parliament. He felt that America must become independent, and he made his case in *Common Sense*.

What Does *Common Sense* Say?

Paine believed that the American colonies could win independence despite a military disadvantage. At the time, the most important part of a country's military was its navy, and Britain had the best navy in the world. However, Paine claimed that America had many advantages over Britain. For example, it was rich in natural resources like trees, which were needed to build ships. Additionally, British soldiers would have to travel a great distance to reach the fighting.

More important was Paine's argument that British rule was unfair. He wanted to create a free society in which decisions were made not by a king or queen, but by the people. The ideas in *Common Sense* were easy to understand, and they still influence American politics today. Because of this, *Common Sense* is an important part of American history.

The ideas were not Paine's alone. He drew from a European intellectual movement called the Enlightenment* that emphasized reason and individualism over tradition. Among the interests of Enlightenment thinkers was a general inquiry into how societies could be fairer. Nobody, however, had yet tried to organize a society based on Enlightenment principles.

Paine helped change that. After winning the Revolution, American society was formed around the sorts of personal freedom for which Enlightenment thinkers argued. While some believed such a system would lead to chaos, America's success proved them wrong. Paine is considered one of the Founding Fathers of the United States because of his pamphlet's role in these political changes.

Those studying Paine should see *Common Sense* as valuable for two reasons. First, it helps us understand the fears and thoughts that average eighteenth-century colonists had about their political situation. It also shows us why even some who were not happy with recent events wanted to stay part of the British Empire.* Second, Paine's writing style influenced the way future political arguments were made. He took the political opinion of elite thinkers and made them accessible to anyone who could read. As the political historian Eric Foner* notes, Paine "communicated a new vision" of government not just to a broad American audience, but to a worldwide audience.[1]

Why Does *Common Sense* Matter?

Common Sense listed reasons in favor of American independence and attacked those who wanted to remain British subjects. As such, the text provides the reader with a sense of the eighteenth-century public's feeling and mood. It can therefore help students understand both history and politics. It can also help explain why freedom is considered to be so important to so many today.

Common Sense was innovative because it made difficult ideas easy to understand. These ideas would outlast the Revolution and become part of everyday politics. For example, Paine's ideas made their way into both the Declaration of Independence* (the statement issued by 13 British colonies to the British Empire in which they declared that they considered themselves independent) and the US Constitution* (the document setting out the rights of American citizens and the nature and obligations of their government). Both documents formed the basis for the American system of government; the Constitution has proven to be enormously influential globally.

Paine also popularized ideas that had previously been understood only by a few well-educated people. For example, he explained that freedom of religion and freedom of speech were not dangerous, as was thought at the time, but would lead to a better world.

Paine's style also showed that it was beneficial for political writing to be easy to read. The pamphlet sold in large numbers, and the war would not have had so much support without it. Additionally, this support allowed American leaders to put these new ideas into place after the war was over. The success of the new American system caused some Europeans to think about making similar changes. The old argument that a free country would be a horrible place looked weak, and people began to want more from their governments. In this way, we can see how Paine's *Common Sense* drastically affected how people throughout the world saw political systems.

NOTES

1   Eric Foner, *Tom Paine and Revolutionary America* (London, New York, and Oxford: Oxford University Press, 1976), XVI.

SECTION 1
INFLUENCES

MODULE 1
THE AUTHOR AND THE
HISTORICAL CONTEXT

KEY POINTS

- *Common Sense* was instrumental in inspiring popular support for independence.

- Paine immigrated in 1774 to America, where he could argue for his ideas to be put into practice.

- The American Revolutionary War* (the military conflict between 13 colonies of the British Empire and the empire's army that led to the formation of the young United States) provided the chance to create a nation based on the principles of the Enlightenment*—a movement in European culture and thinking towards rationality and individualism.

Why Read This Text?

Thomas Paine first published *Common Sense* in 1776. His pamphlet argues that the political and economic union of America and Britain "sooner or later must have an end."[1] Paine critiques Britain's hereditary monarchy*—a system in which sovereign power is inherited by succeeding generations of the same family—and asserts that it is impractical for a small, distant island to govern a continent. He claimed that Britain had inflicted economic and social injustices upon the colonists that were an affront to their personal freedoms.

While many in America accepted that grievances existed between Britain and the colonies, some believed that reconciliation was possible. However, Paine argued that "everything that is right or natural pleads for separation,"[2] and insisted that independence was the

> **❝ Everything that is right or natural pleads for separation. ❞**
> Thomas Paine, *Common Sense*

best course of action. His arguments led to a notable shift in the attitudes of colonists, who began to support revolution in much larger numbers. It should be noted that the primary purpose of *Common Sense* was propaganda. That is, it was not written to provide unbiased information, but rather to convince its audience that Paine was right.

Paine's text offers a brief summary of eighteenth-century political ideas and helps make contemporary political thought easy to understand. Additionally, *Common Sense* helps us understand how the American Revolution succeeded. This is important because the revolution influenced Western political systems in ways that still reverberate today.

Author's Life
Paine was born in England in 1734 to a Quaker* father and an Anglican mother. His early life was undistinguished. Until he was 13 he attended grammar school,* where he received a basic education. His first marriage ended tragically, when his wife and daughter died during childbirth. Paine's second marriage to Elizabeth Olive lasted only four years, and they formally separated in 1774. His business ventures, such as his tobacco shop, also failed.

Paine's first notable experiment with writing came while working at the Custom and Excise Office in London. He wrote a 21-page pamphlet, *The Case of the Officers of Excise*, in which he argued for better working conditions and an increased salary. He was dismissed from this post shortly after its publication.

Paine's life changed when he was introduced to the American political theorist and scientist Benjamin Franklin* in September 1774.

Little is known about this meeting, but Paine set sail for Philadelphia almost immediately after it. He arrived on November 30 and soon became a citizen. Franklin had given Paine a letter of recommendation—an important endorsement at the time. By January 1775, Paine was employed as the editor of a periodical called the *Pennsylvania Magazine*. Here, he immersed himself in American politics and developed his unique style.

Author's Background

America was still a sovereign territory of Great Britain when Paine arrived in 1774. It was also in the midst of a crisis. Britain and France had fought for control of America in what was known in Europe as the Seven Years War,* and though Britain had won, the war had been expensive. As a consequence, Britain imposed taxes on the colonies to help pay its debts. The colonists were outraged that the government could tax them without their consent, especially given that they had been denied representation in the British Parliament.

The political situation deteriorated further after the Boston Tea Party* of 1773, in which colonists boarded three British ships in Boston Harbor and threw the consignment of tea overboard. The British response was to pass a series of five laws, called the Coercive Acts,*[3] which were designed to punish the colonies and reestablish control over the territories. Massachusetts, one of the more rebellious states, was targeted in particular. For instance, the acts closed Boston's port, gave direct control of the Massachusetts government to a British-appointed governor, gave the governor the right to insist that accused government officials be tried in Great Britain, and permitted the governor to house troops in unoccupied buildings.

Unsurprisingly, the new laws provoked outrage: the colonists referred to them as the "Intolerable Acts." As a result, the First Continental Congress* was organized, in which representatives from 12 of the 13 colonies (Georgia did not attend) met in Philadelphia from September to October 1774. Coincidentally, this was almost exactly when Paine arrived in the city.

The congress sent a petition to Britain's king, George III,* asking him to address their grievances with the Coercive Acts and various other issues. After the petition was rejected, the Second Continental Congress* met in May 1775 to prepare for the war effort that many, though not all, now saw as inevitable.

The battles of Lexington and Concord* had been fought on April 19, 1775, and these first conflicts effectively began the American Revolutionary War. On July 4, 1776, the Second Continental Congress issued the Declaration of Independence,* which declared that the 13 colonies were no longer part of the British Empire.

NOTES

1   Thomas Paine, *Common Sense* (New York: Dover Publications Inc., 1997), 22.

2   Paine, *Common Sense,* 22.

3   Only four of the five acts were in direct response to the general sense of rebellion. The fifth was related to the borders of Quebec.

MODULE 2
ACADEMIC CONTEXT

KEY POINTS

- *Common Sense* discussed what should be done about the political crises unfolding in the American colonies.

- Thinkers of the Enlightenment*—the current of European thought that increasingly stressed rationality and individualism—emphasized the rights of the individual over the power of the state.

- Paine was self-taught and had no formal education in political philosophy.

The Work in its Context

In *Common Sense*, Thomas Paine appealed to a sense of national pride that existed in Britain's colonies in the eighteenth century. Although his writing reflected "the consensus opinion of his Enlightenment peers,"[1] Paine's goal was not to educate but to inspire political change. He wrote so that the common colonist could grasp his meaning, mixing straightforward arguments with biblical references, and appealing to how colonists felt about the political climate.

Paine chose not to mention Enlightenment philosophers such as the British political philosopher John Locke,* the Genevan political philosopher Jean-Jacques Rousseau,* and the French political philosopher and writer Voltaire,* and others more immediate to Paine's circle, such as the American political theorist and scientist Benjamin Franklin.* However, it is easy to see how he was influenced by these thinkers, given what they contributed to eighteenth-century thought.

> ❝ But where, says some, is the King of America? I'll tell you friend, he reigns above and doth not make havoc of mankind like the Royal Brute of Britain. ❞
>
> Thomas Paine, *Common Sense*

Locke is often considered the father of modern liberalism,* and, along with Voltaire, argued for the rights of the individual and the separation of church and state. Rousseau's writing on social inequality and political systems would influence both the American Revolution* (in which the young United States forcibly took its independence from the British Empire*) and the French Revolution* (in which French citizens rose up to overturn the social order, overthrowing the monarchy and instituting a republic).

Ideas about individual rights and freedoms were not immediately accessible to the average person in the eighteenth century. The American colonies were subject to the king of England, and though his power was not absolute, colonists were still limited in what they could do and say. Unlike today, no real alternative to this system of government had been attempted. As such, it was difficult for those in favor of individual liberty to answer those who argued that individual liberties would lead to anarchy.*

Overview of the Field

The intellectual climate of the time was volatile, as Enlightenment thinkers were challenging existing beliefs about religion, government, and individual rights. Like Voltaire, Paine was a deist,* meaning that he believed that reason rather than tradition should be the foundation for belief in God. He also believed that reason and not tradition should be the basis of government. Though he did state these claims explicitly in *Common Sense,* it is still possible to see the influences of Enlightenment thinkers in the subtext of the pamphlet.

An idea central to *Common Sense,* and to all Enlightenment political thought, is the social contract*—the idea, established by the English philosopher Thomas Hobbes,* that human nature is governed by reason, and that there is a limit to the number of rights citizens should consent to lose for the sake of good governance; Hobbes believed that human beings would live in chaos unless subject to strong authoritative governments like monarchies.

Paine agreed with Hobbes that some form of government was necessary for civil society, but he strongly disagreed about how much was required. Paine argued not only that were men free, equal, and independent, but also that their only king was God, who reigned above and "doth not make havoc of mankind like the Royal Brute of Britain."[2]

John Locke was another important influence on Paine. Locke believed that human nature was governed by reason, and he argued for a form of government in which people voluntarily abandoned personal liberties in order to create a civil society. Locke had argued that people should give up fewer rights than Hobbes thought they should, and Paine took this even further. According to Paine, citizens should give up as few rights as possible—and some rights could not be given up at all, not even by choice.

Although Paine recognized that societies needed leaders, he wanted a presidential system,* in which the leader is elected by the people, and not a hereditary monarchy,* in which authority stays within a family and is passed from generation to generation. Furthermore, he believed that the presidency should be both temporary and limited in power.[3] In *Common Sense*, Paine argued that his ideas should be put into place. The pamphlet was not just a contribution to philosophical debate.

Academic Influences

While we have seen that Enlightenment thinking influenced Paine, it is possible to look more closely at his principles. He believed in liberalism, a political philosophy that emphasizes freedom, equality, and regularly contested elections. He was also influenced by republicanism,* an ideology that rejects the notion that the head of state should be a hereditary position, such as that of a king or other monarch. Finally, he was a radical,* which at the time referred to those who wished to break with England in order to create a fairer society. Today, it should be noted, radicalism has come to mean any form of extreme ideology. Paine may also have learned a great deal from Benjamin Franklin, who was a politician of considerable influence, as well as a polymath* (that is, his expertise spanned several fields of knowledge).

Paine's Enlightenment peers had been struggling with how best to organize society for some time. Hobbes had felt that without an authoritative ruler, the strong would dominate or enslave the weak. As a result, he thought that life was the only inalienable, or guaranteed, right that people had. Locke was less extreme. He wrote that people had a range of incontestable rights, but that they still had to trade some for security and peace.

According to Paine, however, Hobbes's monarch was a tyrant, and Locke's constitutional monarchy,* in which the power of the monarch was limited by a constitution, was not much better. Paine melded these ideas with more modern thinking, such as that of Jean-Jacques Rousseau, who argued for democratic rule. Though this does not seem radical today, it contradicted the common wisdom of the day.

NOTES

1   Craig Nelson, *Thomas Paine: His Life, His Time and the Birth of Modern Nations* (London: Profile Books, 2007), 8.

2   Thomas Paine, *Common Sense* (New York: Dover Publications Inc., 1997), 31.

3   Paine, *Common Sense*, 30.

MODULE 3
THE PROBLEM

KEY POINTS

- Paine wanted to guarantee the rights of the individual above all else.
- In most European countries, the individual was less important than loyalty to one's king or nation.
- Paine made it possible for anyone to understand the debate over individual rights.

Core Questions

Thomas Paine's *Common Sense* tried to answer two core questions. First, was independence from Britain desirable? Second, was it achievable?

Paine intended his pamphlet to serve as propaganda; he believed "yes" was the answer to both questions and made no attempt to offer a balanced discussion. He began writing shortly after the American Revolution* began, although at the time, many, including some in the Continental Congress,* still hoped for reconciliation. This is why these core questions were so important: Paine's primary purpose was to convince both the masses and American leaders that independence was the correct course of action.

Paine said British rule amounted to tyranny. He was less clear on whether independence could be achieved. At the time, defeat was a serious possibility. Given what we know now, it is easy to miss how much Paine's argument was a monumental gamble. That the gamble paid off remains one of the more compelling reasons why *Common Sense* has endured.

> ❝ As in absolute governments the king is law so too in free countries the law ought to be king. ❞
>
> Thomas Paine, *Common Sense*

The Participants

Although *Common Sense* does not refer to specific political or philosophical theories, Paine's intellectual influences are clear. One important thinker whose ideas we find reflected in the pamphlet is the English philosopher John Locke.*

Locke's concept of a civilized society was based on natural rights,* or rights that should be guaranteed to all people, and social contract theory,* which was the idea that some liberties should be given up for the sake of a peaceful, just society.

Paine took Locke's belief that only consent could "give a man permanent membership of society," and expressed it in language that was deliberately inflammatory.[1] For example, Paine wrote that independence meant "no more than, whether we shall make our own laws or, whether the King, the greatest enemy this continent hath or can have shall tell us 'there shall be no laws but such as I like'."[2] Most Enlightenment* texts were not nearly so provocative, because they were directed at an intellectual audience and their authors, who feared arrest, tended to be more cautious.

Not every Enlightenment thinker believed in the same version of social contract theory, and Paine drew from a range of sources. Another of his influences was the philosopher Jean-Jacques Rousseau,* who was born in Geneva, in what is now Switzerland. In *Du Contrat social*, Rousseau claimed that it was important for citizens to obey the law for the collective good of society.[3] Like Rousseau, Paine believed in the importance of laws based on reason, writing that "as in absolute governments the king is law so too in free countries the law ought to be king."[4]

He differed from Rousseau in that he valued individual rights over the collective good. Paine dismissed the question of what rights colonists should give up entirely, since he did not think English law was legitimate:"[you] that oppose independence now [you] know not what [you] do," he wrote;"[you] are opening a door to eternal tyranny by leaving vacant the seat of government."[5]

In making this statement, he further radicalized* what were already extreme ideas. *Common Sense* thus attacks British rule both by asking what rights citizens should give up to their rulers, and who should be permitted to rule in the first place.

The Contemporary Debate

When Paine published *Common Sense* in 1776, the intellectual battlefield included a volatile mix of Enlightenment ideas, traditional thinking, and realpolitik* ideas (that is, ideas governed by practical concerns rather than moral considerations). Paine drew on this debate, often taking radical ideas and making them even more extreme.

For example, John Locke believed that monarchs should have their power limited by a constitution. Paine took this further, ridiculing even the concept of a constitutional monarchy:* "Why is the constitution of England sickly, but because monarchy hath poisoned the republic, the crown hath engrossed the commons?"[6] Similarly, the French philosopher Voltaire* believed that England was freer than France because of its constitutional monarchy. Paine, however, openly dismissed the idea that English liberties had any real substance.

Even supporters of independence such as the politician John Adams,* who was to be the second president of the United States, thought *Common Sense* was too radical. According to Adams, Paine tended to resort to false dichotomies, or claiming that only two choices exist when in reality there are many possibilities. In *Thoughts on Government* (1776), Adams rejected Paine's idea that the country could be governed by a single legislative body. He wrote that people could not "be long free, nor ever happy, whose government is in one assembly."[7]

To understand *Common Sense* today, the reader must have some understanding of Enlightenment thought. It is important to remember that while Paine borrowed ideas, he took the time to trace their origins, as he wanted his pamphlet to be simple and accessible.

Finally, one reason why Paine's ideas were often more extreme than those whose work he drew on was the context in which he wrote. Those writing in Europe could afford to make abstract arguments. Paine's ideas had to be immediately applied to the volatile political situation in the colonies; there was so very little time for debate.

NOTES

1   John Locke, *Two Treatises of Government*, ed. Peter Laslett (Cambridge: Cambridge University Press, 1988), 111.

2   Thomas Paine, Common Sense (New York: Dover Publications Inc., 1997), 27.

3   Christopher D. Wraight, *Rousseau's* The Social Contract*: A Reader's Guide* (New York: Continuum, 2008), 33.

4   Paine, Common Sense, 31–2.

5   Paine, Common Sense, 33.

6   Paine, Common Sense, 17.

7   John Adams, *Thoughts on Government*, accessed November 7, 2013, http://www.constitution.org/jadams/thoughts.htm.

THE AUTHOR'S CONTRIBUTION

KEY POINTS

- Paine believed that the only interest government should serve was the will of the people.

- By putting Enlightenment* ideas into practice, Paine contributed significantly to the formation of the United States.

- Paine understood the need to translate abstract philosophical ideas into practical ones in order to cause political change.

Author's Aims

In writing *Common Sense*, Thomas Paine was aware of the limits of his intended audience. The philosophical ideas that informed his work were not familiar to the average person in 1776—and nor were they easily explained. Thus his text was not a philosophical treatise but a call for political action. It was written clearly and concisely, avoiding complex metaphors and intricate arguments.

Because literacy was uncommon in eighteenth-century New England, there were also restrictions on the pamphlet's length. *Common Sense* was intended to be read aloud at public gatherings, which would have been difficult had it been long. This was one reason why the pamphlet was revolutionary: its briefness and use of plain speech allowed common people to understand complex political and philosophical ideas.

Called "the first American self-help book … for those who could not imagine life without a monarch,"[1] *Common Sense* became an instant best seller,[2] stirring opinion across the continent and, perhaps

> ❝ The tremendous impact of Paine's writings in Europe and America has never been adequately explained, and Paine's relationship to the expansion of popular participation in politics—a major achievement in the Age of Revolution—is still not clear. ❞
>
> Eric Foner, *Tom Paine and Revolutionary America*

more importantly, boosting morale in the Continental army commanded by George Washington—a man who was to be the first president of the young United States.

Approach

Paine rejected the notion that reconciliation with Great Britain was possible, even if some still desired it. Two aspects of Paine's response to those who opposed independence are noteworthy.

First, he drew from Enlightenment thinkers who believed that political systems should be based on reason, not tradition. Second, he knew a great deal about contemporary American politics and was able to apply Enlightenment ideas clearly to them. Paine's innovation was to ask not *if* the colonies should become independent, but *how*. In his view, continued British rule was not an option.

While most political philosophers had to create hypothetical examples of how their ideas might work, Paine was able to draw upon real-world events that were already unpopular, such as the Coercive Acts*—laws imposed by the British government on the state of Massachusetts and intended to punish the colonists for behavior considered to be insubordinate (that is, rebellious). His ideas were therefore not abstract; they were applicable to current affairs.

While thinkers in Europe were asking questions about what rights people should be allowed, Paine pointed to those that were already being denied or abused. This combination of an intellectual analysis and an appeal to emotion struck a chord with readers from all over the continent.

Contribution in Context

Paine was the inheritor of an eclectic set of ideas originated by figures such as the Genevan Enlightenment philosopher Jean-Jacques Rousseau,* "a man much esteemed by Paine,"[3] who had already argued that democracy was the best form of government. Rousseau had developed his thinking by studying the British political philosophers John Locke* and Thomas Hobbes.* The historian Christopher Hitchens* points out that it is "not known whether Paine ever read Hobbes, and he always denied having read John Locke's essay on *Civil Government*,"[4] but we can still see their influences in *Common Sense*.

Paine was able to apply these ideas directly to the plight of the colonies; in this way, he was not only critiquing British misrule but also the British political system. Unlike Locke and Hobbes, Paine rejected the idea of a king—even one limited by a constitution—and opted instead for a system that called for leaders to be chosen and removed from office on a regular basis.

It is difficult to know exactly where to position Paine within academic thought. In *Common Sense*, the stance he takes against monarchy allows us to identify him as a republican,* and his emphasis on equality, freedom, and individual rights suggests that he was a liberal* and a radical.* However, it is only by examining his later works, such as *The Rights of Man** (1791), that we can definitively say that he was influenced by social contract theory.* In *The Rights of Man*, Paine applied existing political theory to the events that had led to the American crisis, and later to the French Revolution.* More importantly, he adapted and combined ideas from multiple sources that fit his vision of freedom.

NOTES

1   Craig Nelson, *Thomas Paine: His Life, His Time and the Birth of Modern Nations* (London: Profile Books, 2007), 84.

2   Thomas Paine, *The Thomas Paine Reader*, ed. Michael Foot and Isaac Kramnick (London: Penguin, 1987), 10.

3   Christopher Hitchens, *Thomas Paine's Rights of Man* (New York: Grove Press, 2006), 95.

4   Hitchens, *Rights of Man*, 106.

SECTION 2
IDEAS

MODULE 5
MAIN IDEAS

KEY POINTS

* *Common Sense* argued that Britain had betrayed its colonies, and that America was morally required to fight for independence.

* Paine showed that the grievances Americans felt toward Britain represented a larger social injustice.

* He wrote in a bold, dramatic style, and persuaded his audience using language they were familiar with.

Key Themes

Common Sense's argument is built on the premise that government "even in its best state is but a necessary evil,"[1] and at its worst is an "intolerable one." As such, Paine begins by describing how governments, in particular monarchies, can be harmful. He argues that American independence is inevitable and insists that without it, British tyranny would continue to cause social injustice. He ties these ideas together by touching upon a philosophical concept that was important to Enlightenment* thinkers: an examination of the "state of nature"* (that is, the hypothetical way in which people would have lived before societies were formed).

Paine's explanation of the social contract*—an idea based on the assumption that human nature is governed by reason, and that people should only trade so many rights for stable government—is subtle.

First, he asks the reader to imagine each person living on his or her own, in a "state of nature." It would be logical for people to want to create a "society,"[2] since, according to Paine, the "strength of one man is so unequal to his wants and his mind so unsuited to perpetual

> **❝** Society in every state is a blessing but government even in its best state is but a necessary evil; in its worst state an intolerable one. **❞**
>
> Thomas Paine, *Common Sense*

solitude."[3] In coming together, people would need to agree upon rules and choose leaders to govern them.

However, Paine writes, the invention of government had been conceived in "dark and slavish times,"[4] and was now "imperfect, subject to convulsions, and incapable of producing what it seems to promise."[5] According to Paine, examples of these "imperfections" include England's unwritten constitution (called "unwritten" because it existed in multiple documents and practices, and not as a single, unified text) and hereditary monarchy,* in which the crown was passed from generation to generation according to tradition. In particular, Paine sees the king as the source of all social injustice.

Paine accuses the British government of crimes stretching back several years. Among these crimes are unfair taxation, lack of representation in the British Parliament, and the bloody battles of Lexington and Concord* and Bunker Hill in 1775, when the Revolutionary army engaged the British army in the colony of Massachusetts, with great loss of life.

In Paine's view, reconciliation would not resolve the colonists' grievances because it would not change the fact that the colonies were ruled by a king. As such, Paine charges those who support reconciliation with "opening a door to eternal tyranny."[6] And because Britain had refused to agree to colonial demands, the only two options Paine allows for are surrender or revolution. From this perspective, war seems inevitable: the colonists' position was intolerable and would not change unless they escaped British rule.

Exploring the Ideas

Paine doesn't just disapprove of the British government's policies. He writes that the very system is corrupt. He denounces the hereditary monarchy as "an insult and an imposition on prosperity,"[7] and reasons that the way to correct the problem is to change the system. This, in Paine's view, is why Americans must become independent: there was no will in Britain to change from a constitutional monarchy,* which they saw as a liberal, workable system.

America would have to break from the mother country herself. Paine writes that the Old World is "overrun with oppression," and freedom has been "hunted from the globe."[8] Paine believed that no amount of negotiation with Britain would change this. It would therefore be necessary to construct a new political system based in part on the beliefs of Enlightenment thinkers such as Thomas Hobbes,* John Locke,* Jean-Jacques Rousseau,* and the Dutch philosopher Hugo Grotius,* who was among the first to introduce the idea of natural individual rights in the seventeenth century.

In asking readers to consider what a state of nature might look like, Paine also asks them to reevaluate the social norms with which they had been raised. Paine claims to draw his form of government from "a principle of nature."[9] He also argues that the state of nature proves that hereditary monarchy is illogical—or, as he put it, turns it "into ridicule by giving mankind an ass for a lion."[10] Furthermore, Paine insists that "men, who look upon themselves [as] born to reign and others to obey, soon grow insolent." For Paine, the logic is clear: there are no kings in nature, and "there should be none in society."[11]

Language and Expression

The key ideas in *Common Sense* are best understood as a series of arguments and counterarguments designed to inspire the public to support revolution. Paine begins by rejecting the idea that government should serve any interest other than that of the people. He is especially critical of hereditary monarchy, especially in the ways it limits individual rights. After citing a series of examples to show that the Bible does not support the idea of kings, Paine launches an all-out attack on British rule, citing the absurdity of an island ruling a continent, let alone much of the world.

Paine's outrage is tempered by his calm, logical support for inalienable, or guaranteed, human rights. By both illustrating the injustice of British rule and highlighting the economic practicality of war, Paine's argument addresses specific colonial concerns while also giving voice to the growing anger that colonists felt at the time.

Paine wrote in dramatic, emotional, and provocative English. He wanted the contemporary reader to understand easily why the colonies should fight for independence from Britain. If the text is difficult to read today, it is because it was written nearly 250 years ago: Paine was not writing for future generations, and modern readers may not be familiar with the political affairs of his time. Still, in arguing for how much power government should have over individuals, he speaks to a political debate still relevant to readers today.

NOTES

1   Thomas Paine, *Common Sense* (New York: Dover Publications Inc., 1997), 3.

2   Paine, *Common Sense,* 3.

3   Paine, *Common Sense,* 3.

4   Paine, *Common Sense,* 5.

5   Paine, *Common Sense,* 5.

6   Paine, *Common Sense,* 32.

7   Paine, *Common Sense,* 12.

8   Paine, *Common Sense,* 33.

9   Paine, *Common Sense,* 5.

10 Paine, *Common Sense,* 12.

11 Paine, *Common Sense,* 33.

MODULE 6
SECONDARY IDEAS

KEY POINTS

- *Common Sense* also suggested that the colonies could both win and profit by the war.
- Paine's argument allowed Americans to question their loyalty to the British king.
- Not all the claims Paine made in *Common Sense* were realistic.

Other Ideas

Although Thomas Paine's primary goal in *Common Sense* is to convince colonists that independence is the best course of action, he makes a number of other important points. He articulates some of the perceived crimes committed under British rule and discusses the current state of the colonies—particularly their military strength.

Readers should be aware that Paine was not writing a textbook and did not feel the need to give details or evidence. For example, Paine refers to the "Massacre at Lexington," without explaining that he is referring to fighting that began in the towns of Lexington and Concord,* Massachusetts, after the British army attempted to destroy colonial military supplies.[1] Similarly, he writes, "Thousands of lives are already ruined by British barbarity,"[2] without mentioning specific incidents.

Paine understood that war with Britain would be expensive and risky, and speaks to these fears. He notes that the colonies were free from debt, and therefore prepared to "repel the forces of all the world."[3] He also said that since America possessed the "largest body of armed and disciplined men of any power under Heaven,"[4] the colonies

> ❝ Through this new language, he communicated a new vision—a utopian image of an egalitarian society— and in so doing ideas surrounding natural rights and republicanism became instantly accessible to all. ❞
>
> Eric Foner, *Tom Paine and Revolutionary America*

could not afford to balk at challenging Britain on purely economical grounds. Britain's strength was its navy, which Paine describes as "formidable," though dismisses, saying "not a tenth part of them are at any one time fit for service."[5] And while the colonies had no warships of their own, Paine was confident that no country was "so happily situated, or so internally capable of raising a fleet as America."[6]

Such ideas were speculative, but also exaggerated. It was true that the British navy was in considerable disarray, but the idea that America could raise a fleet to compete with it was absurd. Readers should also note that war between Britain and the colonies would mostly mean fighting on land, so Paine's claims that America could raise a fleet to repel the British navy ultimately did not matter.

Exploring the Ideas

While America's successful revolution vindicated Paine's insistence that the colonists need "fear no external enemy,"[7] some of the claims he made were questionable. Paine seems at times more concerned with using dramatic, inflammatory language to incite colonists to support war than with making reasonable points.

For example, his analysis of colonial military capabilities can only be explained as ignorance, reckless overconfidence, or an outright lie. While it is true that the British navy was not able to blockade the entire coast, and that punitive attacks, like the burning of Falmouth,* Massachusetts, were annoyances, the reality was that in 1776 the American navy was practically nonexistent.[8] It was not until 1778, when France, Spain, and the Netherlands entered the war on America's behalf, that British naval superiority was contested.

Paine also avoided describing the specific events he cites as evidence of British tyranny, such as the battles at Lexington and Concord.* Instead, he uses broad sweeping statements to critique Britain. England's constitution, which was not a single document but a group of documents and policies, was fit only for "Dark and slavish times;"[9] King George III* was the descendent of a "French Bastard;"[10] and, more importantly, Britain had heaped unforgivable injuries upon the colonies.

Overlooked

Towards the end of *Common Sense*, Paine focuses his arguments on the Quakers.* He does this for two reasons. First, Paine's father was a Quaker (though his mother was not), and this connection gave him insight into the group's opinions. Second, and more importantly, Paine was living and writing in Philadelphia, where there were many Quakers, and it was logical to ask for their support. Paine may not have anticipated that *Common Sense* would be read so widely.

In this part of the pamphlet, Paine adopts a more diplomatic tone, insisting that "our plan is for peace forever. We are tired of contention with Britain and can see no real end to it but separation."[11]

Paine knew that the Quaker religion was based on pacifism,* or opposition to war and violence. Though Quakers initially supported resistance to Britain—they had, for example, opposed the crown's taxation policies—they were alarmed by the escalating violence on both sides. Events such as the Boston Tea Party* (a political protest in the course of which activists threw a shipload of tea into Boston harbor in protest at taxes Americans were obliged to pay without representation in the British Parliament) and the passage of the Coercive Acts* (punitive laws imposed by Britain in retaliation for American rebelliousness) suggested that war was inevitable. Paine didn't think that Quakers would support war with Britain, which is why he addressed them directly—but he believed that, while they would not bear arms, that did not mean that they were required to remain neutral.

NOTES

1   Thomas Paine, *Common Sense* (New York: Dover Publications Inc., 1997), 26.

2   Paine, *Common Sense*, 26.

3   Paine, *Common Sense,* 34.

4   Paine, *Common Sense,* 34.

5   Paine, *Common Sense,* 38.

6   Paine, *Common Sense,* 36.

7   Paine, *Common Sense*, 39.

8   Stephen Howarth, *To Shining Sea: A History of the United States Navy, 1775–1998* (Norman: University of Oklahoma Press, 1991), 6.

9   Paine, *Common Sense,* 5.

10 Paine, *Common Sense,* 33.

11 Paine, *Common Sense,* 53.

MODULE 7
ACHIEVEMENT

KEY POINTS

- Paine's pamphlet convinced many Americans to favor independence.
- *Common Sense* was written to inflame public opinion.
- Paine played less of a role in shaping the United States than in helping it achieve independence.

Assessing the Argument

It is clear that in *Common Sense* Thomas Paine wanted to inspire the colonial masses to support and fight for independence. As such, Paine maintains an outraged and incendiary tone throughout. In addition, he employs two broad tactics to persuade his audience. First, Paine uses economic, moral, and theological evidence to justify his position. Second, he uses these same types of evidence to refute arguments against independence.

It is unclear, however, how much Paine hoped to influence events after the American Revolution.* *Common Sense* certainly does not offer a full, coherent plan for creating a system of government. Paine does suggest some specifics, such as term limits for government officials and presidential elections, but we cannot be sure if he meant these as a blueprint, or if he simply wanted to show colonists that there were alternatives to hereditary monarchies.*

Ultimately, Paine did not contribute directly to the form of the United States government. Nevertheless, he achieved his primary goal when the colonies won their revolution. Paine's claims that the colonies would succeed in their war made him seem prophetic.

> **❝ We have it in our power to begin the world over again. ❞**
> Thomas Paine, *Common Sense*

Achievement in Context

The success of *Common Sense* must be seen as connected to the success of the American Revolutionary War. More, it was written and structured according to what Paine thought would persuade the average colonist. We should also note that Paine's text was directly linked to the events of the crisis in the American colonies, and it probably would not have been published under different circumstances.

Paine's fame lasted because of the colonial victory. Having inspired public support for revolution, Paine did not stop writing about his ideas. Although he addressed the specific situation in America, he also believed his vision was universal, arguing that it was within America's power to "begin the world over again."[1] And indeed, the Revolution that he helped inspire was a major historical event; it contributed, for example, to the French Revolution* that began shortly after, in 1789.

Paine's pamphlet also interested academics, particularly those who studied theology. For example, *Common Sense* attacks the idea that monarchs were divinely appointed. In France, the attack on hereditary monarchy had literal consequences in the execution of the French king, Louis XVI,* in 1793. Similarly, the separation of religion and politics, a foundation of the new American government, has since become important throughout the Western world.

Common Sense is also one of the cornerstones of American political literature. Paine's fiery prose style set the tone for the American Revolution, and for future American political writers. He continued to write this way in his later pamphlets, such as *The American Crises.* He was "aware that he was creating a new style of writing,"[2] and that "most writers in the eighteenth century believed that to write for a mass audience meant to sacrifice refinement for coarseness and triviality."[3] *Common Sense*'s success showed that this was not true.

Limitations

Paine's contemporaries, such as the US's second president, John Adams,* expressed outrage that "history is to ascribe the American Revolution to Thomas Paine,"[4] and attributed more influence to the likes of the political activist Joseph Hewes,* an important signatory of the Declaration of Independence.* *Common Sense* should nevertheless be viewed as a work of immense importance—both for its role in political change, and for its influence on political writing.

Over time, the ideas in *Common Sense* spread. Paine's thinking found its way into both the Declaration of Independence and the US Constitution,* documents on which the history of the United States as an independent and free nation are instituted. More importantly, Paine's ideas endured beyond the Revolution, both because Enlightenment* principles were becoming widely accepted, and because Paine's writing style was so accessible.

Prior to *Common Sense*'s publication in 1776, political writing was mainly directed toward the intellectual elite. Paine's style changed that. According to the University of Virginia professor of history Sophia Rosenfeld,* the effectiveness of "common sense" as a political weapon could be "measured by its many opposition imitators, who seized upon the form's commercial as well as polemical potential."[5] That is, we can see that Paine's style was influential because it had many imitators who valued it as a tool for communicating with the general public. Paine's style became a "commonplace polemical tool in a bitterly fought struggle over the future of politics"[6] because, politicians learned, the language in which a message was delivered was as important as the message itself—perhaps more so.

Thus Paine's text began a new tradition in writing about politics. As the Australian political theorist John Keane* points out, democratic revolution required a "prior democratic revolution in prose."[7] Paine's use of plain language would later be used to great effect in political speeches, such as those of Franklin D. Roosevelt,* who served as president of the United States from 1933 to 1945. Roosevelt channeled Paine when he affirmed "the nation's commitment to defeat fascism and make freedom universal."[8] In saying "make freedom universal," Roosevelt reminded Americans of their heritage.

Paine's belief that America's cause was the world's cause, and that freedom and justice were universal principles, has become part of the American psyche, and Roosevelt used this to influence his audience. Thus we can see that *Common Sense* has had a lasting impact on American political expression from speechwriting to propaganda.

NOTES

1   Thomas Paine, *Common Sense* (New York: Dover Publications Inc., 1997), 51.

2   Eric Foner, *Tom Paine and Revolutionary America* (London, New York, and Oxford: Oxford University Press, 1976), 85.

3   Foner, *Tom Paine and Revolutionary America*, 85.

4   John Adams, *To Thomas Jefferson, vol. 10* of *The Works of John Adams, Second President of the United States: With a Life of the Author, Notes and Illustrations, by His Grandson Charles Francis Adams* (Boston: Little, Brown, 1856), accessed September 22, 2013, http://oll.libertyfund.org/title/2127/193637/3103690.

5   Sophia Rosenfeld, *Common Sense: A Political History* (Cambridge, MA: Harvard University Press, 2011), 44.

6   Rosenfeld, *Common Sense, 54.*

7   John Keane, *Tom Paine: A Political Life* (London, New York, and Berlin: Bloomsbury, 2009), 295.

8   Roosevelt quoted in Harvey J. Kaye, *Thomas Paine and the Promise of America* (New York: Hill & Wang, 2005), 195.

MODULE 8
PLACE IN THE AUTHOR'S WORK

KEY POINTS

- Paine believed that man had certain natural rights,* and that God did not interfere with humanity.

- *Common Sense* includes Paine's philosophical views—but its purpose is to convince America to go to war.

- The text made Paine a celebrity and cemented his role in American history.

Positioning

Common Sense was Thomas Paine's first significant work. His earlier political writing, such as the 1772 pamphlet *The Case of the Officers of Excise*,[1] was more limited in scope, and perhaps produced out of self-interest. The essay "Observations on the Military Character of Ants"—a satire in which red ants, symbolizing the British army, deprived brown ants of their natural rights—appeared in the July 1775 issue of the *Pennsylvania Magazine*. Paine used a pseudonym, Curioso,[2] because of libel laws,* which made it illegal to criticize the government or to incite contempt for the monarch. For the same reason, *Common Sense* was initially published anonymously, though it did not take long for its author to be identified. It is difficult to overstate how important the pamphlet was to Paine's career; it "burst from the press with an effect which has rarely been produced by types and paper in any age or country,"[3] and Paine became a celebrity.

Common Sense was written as a call to arms. The battles of Lexington and Concord* (April 1775) and Bunker Hill (June 1775) had already taken place by the time it was published in January 1776, and the point of no return occurred only five months after, when the

> **❝ Paine's work burst from the press with an effect which has rarely been produced by types and paper in any age or country. ❞**
>
> Daniel Conway Moncure, *The Life of Thomas Paine*

Declaration of Independence* was signed. Between 1773 and 1776, Paine wrote 16 pamphlets collectively titled *The American Crises*. Written in a similar style to *Common Sense*, they were designed to improve colonial morale and spread Paine's philosophical ideas.

Integration

Common Sense was instrumental in gaining public support for the Revolution.* It also established Paine's reputation and helped popularize his later works, in which he explained his ideas more thoroughly.

These later texts affirmed his unwavering stance against monarchies and his commitment to liberty. He remained a liberal* (in the sense of one committed to equality and regular elections) and a deist,* believing that a faith in God should be founded on reason rather than tradition. He would expand upon these and many other ideas in his seminal work *The Rights of Man* (1791). The book became popular because of Paine's reputation, and it is considered his most important contribution to political philosophy.

Significance

Though *Common Sense* made Paine a celebrity, it did not contain fully articulated versions of Paine's ideas. Paine's later works were true academic texts and influential in their own right, though readers should note that their publication was only guaranteed by the success of *Common Sense*. Paine's pamphlet took on historical significance because America had won its independence and created a government based on the liberal principles he had written about; his later works built on this reputation.

Paine wrote *The Rights of Man* because he was inspired by the French Revolution,* during which the French monarch, Louis XVI,* was executed and several constitutions were drafted. In it, Paine attacks hereditary succession and a monarchy whose "despotism resident in the person of the King divides and subdivides itself into a thousand shapes and forms."[4] His other important text, *The Age of Reason* (1794), is primarily concerned with religion and makes an argument for deism. This was a departure from his other works in that it risked religious controversy. By comparison, where *Common Sense* contained religious sentiments, these were only to justify the war for independence. It should be noted that these ideas were an extension of Enlightenment thinking; they were not Paine's originally.

NOTES

1   Thomas Paine, *The Writings of Thomas Paine*, vol. 4, ed. Moncure Daniel Conway (New York: G.P. Putnam's Sons, 1894), accessed December 8, 2014, http://oll.libertyfund.org/titles/1083.

2   Edward Larkin, "Inventing an American Public: Thomas Paine, the *Pennsylvania Magazine*, and American Revolutionary Discourse," *Early American Literature* 33, no. 3 (1998): 250–76.

3   Moncure Daniel Conway, *The Life of Thomas Paine: With a History of His Literary, Political and Religious Career in America, France, and England; to Which Is Added a Sketch of Paine by William Cobbett,* vol. 1 (New York and London: G.P. Putnam and Sons, 1894), 25.

4   Thomas Paine, *The Rights of Man* (New York: Dover Publications Inc., 1999), 14.

SECTION 3
IMPACT

MODULE 9
THE FIRST RESPONSES

KEY POINTS

- Contemporaries criticized *Common Sense* for its superficial arguments and provocative style.

- Candidus,* a writer who believed that the colonies should remain loyal to Britain, argued that the rebels would be more tyrannical than the king.

- Even those who agreed with Paine that the colonies should become independent did not always agree about the form the new government should take.

Criticism

The primary critics of Thomas Paine's *Common Sense* were loyalists,* colonials who wanted to remain part of the British Empire. They saw the pamphlet as a dangerous work composed by "a writer whose powerful literary style was crucial to disseminating its irrational and dangerous arguments."[1] Loyalists often wrote that conditions in the society Paine envisioned would be worse, and that the rebels would more ruthless than the British. For example, a writer who used the pseudonym Candidus*—a man historians believe to be the Scottish-born military officer James Chalmers—warned that if the colonials won the war against the British, they would persecute the loyalists with "more unrelenting virulence than the professed advocates of arbitrary power."[2]

Loyalist critics such as the poet Jonathan Odell from New Jersey came from a variety of social backgrounds,[3] and were united by political views that cut across social and geographical divides. Their arguments, however, had little impact on the American Revolution;*

> ❝ [*Common Sense* is] a poor, ignorant, malicious, short-sighted, crapulous mass. ❞
>
> John Adams, *The Works of John Adams*

the colonies declared their independence soon after *Common Sense* was published, just as Paine insisted they must, and the loyalist position rapidly became shaky.

Responses

The second edition of *Common Sense* was published in February 1776. In it, Paine addresses his critics directly. He claims that he delayed publication of the new edition because he was waiting for a "refutation of the doctrine of Independence,"[4] but that "no answer hath yet appeared."[5] This shows the contempt he felt for his critics' position.

Paine did not respond to critics by name or focus on specific disagreements. However, we can guess from his writing which criticisms he felt needed to be answered. For example, he responded to critiques of his anonymity by saying, "who the author of this production is, is wholly unnecessary,"[6] and, because he took accusations of partisanship seriously, he insisted that he was "unconnected with any party and under no sort of influence public or private."[7]

Paine was also critiqued for the alternatives to monarchy he offered. Paine argued that monarchy had "laid the world in 'blood and ashes',"[8] and he felt a similar contempt for England's unwritten constitution. However, critics attacked his alternative, a form of republicanism,* in which all citizens had a say in government. First, they noted that it had already been attempted in the "Protectorate"* of the English revolutionary general and political leader Oliver Cromwell* in the period between 1649 and 1658 when England was a republic. Loyalists also pointed out that Cromwell had himself become a tyrant.

Second, according to John Adams,* Paine's system was no better than a monarchy because it preserved power "in a single sovereign body."[9] Adams, who would become the second president of the United States, agreed with the "necessity of independence and America's ability to maintain it,"[10] but disagreed about what form the new nation's government should take. He dismissed Paine's idea of a direct assembly, in which all people had a say in laws that were passed, as unworkable.[11]

Conflict and Consensus

Since its purpose had been to call for revolution, there was no need for a third edition of *Common Sense* after the war began in earnest. We can therefore only understand the later criticisms of the text based on which of its suggestions were rejected when the new government was formed. Though Paine's vision did resemble what was eventually created, many of his ideas were significantly altered.

Adams—who later referred to *Common Sense* as a "poor, ignorant, malicious, short-sighted, crapulous mass"[12]—felt that "whether Paine knew it or not, his stubborn appeal to undivided popular sovereignty helped to drag republican politics a few yards towards democracy."[13] Adams saw himself as "keeping apart the conflicting ideas of republicanism and democracy,"[14] and he believed that Paine's popular sovereignty, or system in which all citizens had a say in government, was a radical and dangerous idea. Adams believed that all forms of government, not just hereditary monarchies,* were apt to abuse power, and that Paine had "forgotten the elementary truth that democracy dangerously concentrates power in the hands of the many."[15] Ultimately, Adams was a central figure in the structure of the new American government, and his opinion carried significant weight.

NOTES

1   Philip Gould, *Writing the Rebellion: Loyalists and the Literature of Politics in British America* (New York: Oxford University Press, 2013), 121.

2   James Chalmers, *Plain Truth: Addressed to the Inhabitants of America, Containing, Remarks on a Late Pamphlet, Entitled Common Sense* (Charleston, SC: Nabu Press, 2014).

3   Cynthia Dublin Edelberg, *Jonathan Odell: The Loyalist Poet of the American Revolution* (Durham, NC: Duke University Press, 1987).

4   Thomas Paine, *Common Sense* (New York: Dover Publications Inc., 1997), 2.

5   Paine, *Common Sense,* 2.

6   Paine, *Common Sense,* 2.

7   Paine, *Common Sense,* 2

8   Paine, *Common Sense*, 16.

9   John Adams quoted in John Keane, *Tom Paine: A Political Life* (London, New York, and Berlin: Bloomsbury, 2009), 125.

10 Keane, *Tom Paine*, 125.

11 Keane, *Tom Paine*, 125.

12 John Adams, *To Thomas Jefferson*, vol. 10 of *The Works of John Adams, Second President of the United States: With a Life of the Author, Notes and Illustrations, by His Grandson Charles Francis Adams,* vol. 10, "*To Thomas Jefferson*" (Boston: Little, Brown, 1856), accessed September 22, 2013, http://oll.libertyfund.org/title/2127/193637/3103690.

13 See Keane, *Tom Paine*, 127.

14 Keane, *Tom Paine*, 126.

15 Keane, *Tom Paine*, 131.

MODULE 10
THE EVOLVING DEBATE

KEY POINTS

* *Common Sense* revolutionized political prose and shaped politics both in the colonies and beyond.
* The pamphlet drew from Enlightenment* philosophical principles.
* The text's focus on individual rights means it is relevant to American political debate today.

Uses and Problems

Thomas Paine drew his ideas from a mix of Enlightenment political theories, especially those that dealt with social contract theory.* Although these ideas had been purely theoretical up to this point, the American Revolutionary War* put them to the test. The most crucial and progressive aspect of Paine's pamphlet was that it took prior thought and used it to inform social and political change.

In short, Paine's pamphlet argued that important Enlightenment ideas were not just abstractions, but key tools informing government.

It is no coincidence that the French Revolution* began in 1789, only six years after the American Revolution ended. The social upheaval in France was informed by the same philosophers that Paine drew from in *Common Sense*, and by the real events in North America, where the newly independent United States had formed a republic (a system based on the idea that nations do not need to be governed by monarchs).

The republic, free of kings and hereditary monarchy,* was perhaps the most powerful idea in *Common Sense*, and Paine expanded upon it in *The Rights of Man* (1791). It is a system that continues to find expression in today's liberal democracies. That said, the formation of

> **"** Men of all ranks have embarked in the controversy, from different motives, and with various designs; but all have been ineffectual and the period of debate is closed. Arms, as the last resource, decide the contest. **"**
>
> Thomas Paine, *Common Sense*

republics is not always free of trouble or resistance. For example, Edmund Burke,* a member of the British Parliament and critic of British colonial policy, was initially a supporter of the French Revolution but soon became horrified by the bloodshed. He rejected notions of natural rights, asking, "Am I to congratulate a Highway man and murderer who has broke prison upon the recovery of his natural rights?"[1]

Schools of Thought

Many of Paine's foundational ideas were borrowed. We have already encountered some of those who originated the important ideas in *Common Sense*, such as the political philosophers Thomas Hobbes,* John Locke,* and Jean-Jacques Rousseau.* Paine's focus on social contract theory, in which people give up some individual rights in order to form a just society, also associates him with thinkers who came later. One such example is Pierre-Joseph Proudhon,* a French politician and liberal social theorist.

Proudhon founded a philosophy called mutualism, which is based on the idea that societies function best when people depend upon one another. Another descendent of the social contract theory school of thought was American political philosopher John Rawls.* Rawls's *A Theory of Justice* (1971) was a controversial but critically acclaimed book about how resources should best be distributed in a society.

It is important to note that *Common Sense* had little effect on the philosophical and academic conversation surrounding social contract theory. It was not, however, intended to: it was *The Rights of Man* that indicated Paine's importance as a political theorist. A more thorough description of Paine's beliefs, *The Rights of Man* "indicates [Paine's] importance in forcing a broadening of the political nation and the democratizing of national politics."[2]

The most important idea in this book is how Paine defines natural rights—that is, rights that are so fundamental that they cannot even be made law (since that would imply that they could be taken away). The emergence of the American nation helped put these ideas into practice and encouraged other societies to model themselves on the social contract.

In Current Scholarship

Today's political scholars recognize Paine's *Common Sense* as a landmark in American and world history. For example, Harvey Kaye,* a political scientist at the University of Wisconsin, writes that Paine "emboldened Americans to turn their colonial rebellion into a revolutionary war, defined the new nation in a democratically expansive and progressive fashion, and articulated an American identity charged with exceptional purpose and promise."[3] Today, Paine's ideas seem so central to our beliefs about justice and individual rights that it is "almost impossible to understand his ideas as the revolution in thinking that they once were."[4]

The Enlightenment ideas that Paine drew on have significantly influenced Western politics, cultures, and governments. By the end of the Cold War*—a period of tension between the United States and the Soviet Union from 1947 to 1991—the world was experiencing what American political scientist Francis Fukuyama* has described as a "liberal revolution"—one that "has broken out of its original beachheads in Western Europe and North America."[5]

The liberalism* that Fukuyama refers to, while not universal, has certainly become widespread in the Western world, and it reflects

Paine's ideas about liberty and government. Few Western countries maintain their hereditary monarchies, and where they have (for example, the United Kingdom), the monarch has been stripped of power. Today, scholars study *Common Sense* to learn about its role in the American Revolutionary War and its effect on political speech and writing.

NOTES

1   Edmund Burke, *Reflections on the Revolution in France* (Oxford: Oxford University Press, 2006), 8.

2   Mark Philip, Introduction to *Rights of Man, Common Sense, and Other Political Writings*, by Thomas Paine (Oxford: Oxford University Press. 2008), xxiii.

3   Harvey J. Kaye, *Thomas Paine and the Promise of America* (New York: Hill & Wang, 2005), 4.

4   Craig Nelson, *Thomas Paine: His Life, His Time and the Birth of Modern Nations* (London: Profile Books, 2007), 10.

5   Francis Fukuyama, *The End of History and the Last Man* (London: Penguin, 2012), 50.

MODULE 11
IMPACT AND INFLUENCE TODAY

KEY POINTS

- *Common Sense* is a landmark in the history of the American Revolutionary War.*

- Although radical for its time, *Common Sense*'s core ideas now seem ordinary.

- Paine's arguments are still relevant today in that governments continue to exert power over their citizens.

Position

Today, Thomas Paine's *Common Sense* is best seen as a historical document. It tells us about the ideas and events that were controversial in 1775, and it also shows us how Enlightenment* principles such as natural rights* informed eighteenth-century political thought. For Paine, tyranny stood in the way of natural rights, and these rights were enshrined in his vision of a free and democratic American state.

The text is also part of the narrative of the American Revolution, and students of history can see how it contributed to the country's formation. Paine played an important role in this narrative, and the text is interesting because of what it can tell us about political writing and propaganda. Additionally, we can see how Paine's ideas are still relevant to today's liberal* democracies. That said, although *Common Sense* is directly related to modern liberal democratic thought, it has been less influential than Paine's later works, particularly *The Rights of Man** (1791).

Interaction

Common Sense's contribution to eighteenth-century political thought was limited in two ways. First, Paine wrote to inflame public

> **❝** The impact of ... *Common Sense* as a political weapon can also be measured by its many Opposition imitators, who seized upon the form's commercial as well as polemical potential. **❞**
>
> Sophia Rosenfeld, *Common Sense: A Political History*

support for independence, not to influence philosophical debate. Additionally, the Declaration of Independence* was signed only a few months after the pamphlet was published; from that point, there was no turning back from war, making much of Paine's argument, therefore, moot.

Second, though Paine was on the "right side of history," the "worldwide liberal revolution" described by the American political theorist Francis Fukuyama* was still several centuries away.[1] It was not until the twentieth century that government by hereditary monarchy* fell out of favor. Similarly, Paine's writing did not have much immediate effect on imperialism*— in which countries exerted power and influence over other countries through diplomacy or military force—though it was one of the grounds on which he critiqued British rule.

That said, Paine's world view ultimately endured. Today's liberal democracies generally allow for the natural rights of man to coexist peacefully with the government at large—an idea true to the spirit of *Common Sense*. In the twenty-first century, few are comfortable with the idea of one nation dominating another, refusing it any representation, and imposing unfair taxes. Additionally, not many people support a return to pre-democratic government. Intellectuals today who entertain such a possibility remain at the fringes of serious academic debate or are considered political extremists. Thus Paine's legacy is reflected in the forms of government that are most common today.

The Continuing Debate

The debate about individual rights continues to evolve today. The Western world has come to revile the idea of a nation that does not guarantee the natural rights of its citizens. One explanation for this is what the French cultural theorist Paul Virilio* calls ideological contamination,* in which new technologies allow ideas to spread faster and further. This is one reason why Western intellectual movements, such as those informed by the Enlightenment, have become so widely appealing.[2]

Today, proponents of liberty and individual rights continue to gain ground, as demonstrated by the recent Arab Spring* (a series of protests, demonstrations, and civil wars that swept through the Middle East in 2010 and 2011). As a result of the Arab Spring, rulers were forced from power in Tunisia, Egypt, Libya, and Yemen, and civil conflicts erupted in Bahrain and Syria. While tyranny still exists in the region, proponents of liberty and rights have gained more prominence.

Exceptions exist, of course. One notable example is the People's Republic of China, a nation struggling to prevent ideological contamination from prompting a reform movement in the country. Some Islamist* sects, like the Taliban,* have reacted to the "perceived threat from liberal Western values,"[3] and rejected the idea of natural rights.

NOTES

1   Francis Fukuyama, *The End of History and the Last Man* (London: Penguin, 2012), 39.

2   Paul Virilio, *The Information Bomb*, trans. Chris Turner (London: Verso, 2005), 15.

3   Fukuyama, *The End of History*, 46.

MODULE 12
WHERE NEXT?

KEY POINTS

- Paine's text remains central to understanding the American Revolution* and is still studied for its dramatic, inflammatory prose.
- *Common Sense* will continue to be seen as one of the main inspirations for American independence.
- *Common Sense* is required reading for those who wish to understand why America went to war with Britain.

Potential

Thomas Paine's *Common Sense* is likely to remain an important and influential text in the future. Although it was not a great philosophical work, its role in inspiring support for independence from Great Britain makes it significant. Furthermore, because *Common Sense* was so widely read, Paine deserves credit for popularizing key Enlightenment* ideas.

Paine's pamphlet is also important in that its ideas found their way into two documents that were foundational to the new United States: the Constitution* and the Declaration of Independence,* in which Thomas Jefferson,* who would become the third president of the United States, emphasized the importance of "natural rights."*

Future Directions

Paine's core ideas will probably not be developed further. They are no longer controversial, and much of what Paine argued for has been widely achieved: the formation of governments that allow their citizens natural rights, an end to hereditary monarchy,* free elections,

> ❝[Paine] emboldened Americans to turn their colonial rebellion into a revolutionary war, defined the new nation in a democratically expansive and progressive fashion, and articulated an American identity charged with exceptional purpose and promise.❞
>
> Harvey J. Kaye, *Thomas Paine and the Promise of America*

and, of course, American independence. In today's liberal* democracies, these ideas fall into what the American communications expert Daniel C. Hallin* describes as the "sphere of consensus,"[1] in that they are rarely questioned.

That said, the pamphlet marks a turning point in history. Paine's plain, accessible writing style is now a common feature of political speech. As for its ideas, the fact that readers now struggle to understand why it was so controversial shows how influential Paine's ideas became; today's liberal democracies fulfill most, if not all, of *Common Sense*'s demands. *Common Sense* also resonates because of its criticism of tyrannical governments. Paine's argument for justice is inspiring, and reminds us that America's cause was, and is, a noble one.

Summary

Common Sense was different from other eighteenth-century political texts because of its accessibility and inflammatory prose. Paine attacked any view that ran counter to his argument. He took the radical* ideas of the English Enlightenment philosopher John Locke*—that monarchs could be replaced if they broke the social contract*—and made them even more extreme. Paine heaped scorn upon the British king, George III,* ridiculed the hereditary system, and ultimately made it acceptable for his readers to disobey British rule.

Common Sense was successful not because of its intellectual achievement, but because Paine grasped what was important to the average colonist. In this sense, it was a masterpiece, and it helped spread Enlightenment principles to the masses. It is important for those who want to understand the Revolutionary War, the formation of the new American government, and how the American system eventually influenced other governments around the world. "The cause of America is in a great measure the cause of mankind,"[2] Paine argued, and, as with so many of his predictions, he was correct.

The creation of the United States has greatly influenced today's liberal democracies.

NOTES

1   Daniel C. Hallin, *The Uncensored War: The Media and Vietnam* (Berkeley: University of California Press, 1989), 116.

2   Thomas Paine, *Common Sense* (New York: Dover Publications Inc., 1997), 2.

GLOSSARY

GLOSSARY OF TERMS

American Revolutionary War (1775–83): a military conflict between Britain and the 13 American colonies, although it eventually drew in France, Spain, and the Netherlands. Also known as the American War of Independence.

Anarchy: general disorder resulting from individuals' unwillingness to recognize authority. Some political thinkers—giving primacy to self-regulating individual freedom and dismissing the need for government—argue in favor of anarchy as a form of social organization.

Arab Spring: a series of violent and nonviolent protests, demonstrations, and civil wars that swept through the Middle East in 2010 and 2011. As a result of the Arab Spring, rulers have been forced from power in Tunisia, Egypt, Libya, and Yemen, and civil wars have erupted in Bahrain and Syria.

Boston Tea Party: an incident on December 16, 1773, in which colonists boarded three British ships in Boston harbor and threw their consignment of tea overboard. This was in response to the Tea Act of 1773, which was part of legislation that both raised revenue and established that Britain could impose taxes on the colonies.

British Empire: a maritime—or naval—empire established between the sixteenth and eighteenth centuries. It comprised colonies and territories such as Canada, Australia, New Zealand, South Africa, India, and what would become the United States.

Burning of Falmouth: an incident in October 1775, when the British navy bombarded the town of Falmouth. Originally located in Massachusetts, the site is now a part of Maine.

Coercive Acts: nicknamed the "Intolerable Acts" by colonists in favor of revolution, these were a series of laws imposed upon Massachusetts that, among other things, placed it under the authority of leaders appointed by the British king, George III.

Cold War (1947–91): a period of tension between the United States and the Soviet Union. It did not result in war between the countries, but was instead carried out through espionage and proxy wars.

Constitutional monarchy: a form of government in which the power of the monarch is limited through the passage of a constitution.

Declaration of Independence: a statement that the 13 colonies no longer considered themselves to be part of the British Empire. The declaration was ratified (that is, officially agreed) at the Second Continental Congress on July 4, 1776.

Deism: the belief that reason rather than tradition should be the foundation for belief in God.

English liberties: limits on the power of kings, such as the right to be tried by a jury and restrictions on the monarch's power to raise taxes.

Enlightenment: a movement in seventeenth- and eighteenth-century Europe that challenged commonly held ideas based in tradition and faith, and tried to advance knowledge through rationality and science.

First Continental Congress: a meeting from September to October 1774 that petitioned King George III for redress of grievances. It included representatives from 12 of the 13 colonies (the state of Georgia did not attend).

French Revolution (1789–99): a period of political and social upheaval that culminated in the execution of King Louis XVI and the drafting of several temporary constitutions.

Grammar school: a type of school. The grammar schools of Paine's times were privately run establishments that taught a limited range of subjects, including the Scriptures, Latin, Greek and mathematics.

Hereditary monarchy: a system of government according to which the crown is passed from one generation to the next, usually through the eldest male heir.

Ideological contamination: a process by which new technologies enable the swift spread of ideas from one location to the next.

Imperialism: a policy in which a country exerts power and influence over other countries through economic policy, diplomacy, or military force.

Islamists: members of any Islamic group that desires political control.

Lexington and Concord: two battles that occurred in April 1775 in towns near Boston. Fighting began when the British army attempted to destroy colonial military supplies and met local resistance.

Libel: a system of laws that, among other things, made it illegal to criticize the government of the day or to incite hatred or contempt of the monarch. Publishing anonymously was a common tactic used to avoid arrest.

Liberalism: a political philosophy that emphasizes freedom, equality, and regularly contested elections.

Loyalists: a faction of colonists who wanted to remain part of the British Empire.

Natural rights: universal and absolute rights with which each individual is born, such as the right to "the pursuit of happiness." These rights are separate from legal rights.

Pacifism: a philosophy that opposes war and violence.

Polymath: someone whose expertise spans several different fields.

Presidential system: a type of government headed by a president who is elected by the people or the people's representatives.

Protectorate: period from 1649 to 1658, when England was a republic and Oliver Cromwell ruled as Lord Protector.

Quakers: a Christian denomination that originated in seventeenth-century England. Opposed to war and violence.

Radicalism: any form of progressive liberal ideology. At the time *Common Sense* was published, radicalism meant those who wanted to break from England to create a fairer society.

Realpolitik: a nineteenth-century term referring to the practical and achievable aspects of political action as opposed to action based on moral or ideological considerations.

Republicanism: an ideology that rejected the notion of hereditary monarchy.

***The Rights of Man*:** Paine's 1791 book, written in response to the French Revolution, which began in 1789, and to Edmund Burke's *Reflections on the Revolutions in France*, which had been critical of the revolution. In it, Paine states that revolution is an acceptable response if the government is incapable or unwilling to guarantee certain basic or "'natural' rights."

Second Continental Congress: a meeting of colonial representatives in May 1775 to organize resistance to the British. This became the acting American government.

Seven Years War (1754–63): a war between Great Britain and France over conflicting trade interests across their respective empires.

Social contract theory: the philosophy that human nature is governed by reason, and that there is a limit to the number of rights people should give up in order to be governed.

Soviet Union, or USSR (1922–91): a federation of communist republics in northern Asia and Eastern Europe. The Union of Soviet Socialist Republics was created from the Russian Empire in the aftermath of the Russian Revolution of 1917. The Soviet Union, then the largest country in the world, became a superpower and rival to the United States during the Cold War.

State of nature: a thought experiment used by philosophers to help describe what life was like before people began to live in groups.

Taliban: an Islamist militant organization that seized power in Afghanistan in 1996 and set out to create an authoritarian Islamic state, sweeping aside personal liberty in the process. For example, television and Internet access were outlawed, and men were ordered to keep their beards at a certain length.

Tea Act of 1773: part of a series of acts designed to raise revenue and establish the principle that Britain had the right to impose taxes on the colonies. The Boston Tea Party was a response to the Tea Act.

US Constitution: the supreme legal document of the United States, ratified at the Second Continental Congress by all 13 states in 1790, it described the type of government the country would have and guaranteed each citizen certain rights and protections.

PEOPLE MENTIONED IN THE TEXT

John Adams (1735–1826) was the second president of the United States and a leading advocate of independence from Britain. Though a supporter of Enlightenment principles, he was highly critical of many of Paine's ideas.

Edmund Burke (1729–97) was an Irish political theorist. He is best known for his book *Reflections on the Revolution in France*.

Candidus was the pseudonym used by the author of a 1776 pamphlet entitled *Plain Truth*. Although nobody knows for sure, the author was probably the Maryland loyalist James Chalmers.

Oliver Cromwell (1599–1658) was an English military and political leader who became the Lord Protector of England after the Civil War (1642–51). After he died, the republic collapsed, and a new king, Charles II, was offered the throne.

Eric Foner (b. 1943) is an American historian and biographer of Thomas Paine. He is best known for his work on political history.

Benjamin Franklin (1706–90) was a scientist, author, and political agitator and one of the Founding Fathers of the United States of America. He helped maintain colonial unity during the war and later served as the first ambassador of the United States to France.

Francis Fukuyama (b. 1952) is an American political scientist whose best-known work, *The End of History and the Last Man*, cites liberal democracy and free-market economics as the ultimate means for organizing society.

King George III (1738–1820) was king of Great Britain and ruler of the American colonies until the Declaration of Independence in 1776. He refused to listen to colonial demands, which ultimately led to the American Revolution.

Hugo Grotius (1583–1645) was a Dutch philosopher who introduced the idea of natural and inalienable individual rights. He helped lay the foundations of social contract theory.

Daniel C. Hallin is a researcher in media and communications at the University of San Diego. He is particularly respected for his work on how the media reflect societal norms.

Joseph Hewes (1730–79) was a Quaker from North Carolina and a signatory of the Declaration of Independence. He was also an active participant in the Continental Congress.

Christopher Hitchens (1949–2011) was a prolific writer and journalist. A self-described socialist, Hitchens took contrary views on many popular historical figures, such as Mother Theresa and Pope Benedict XVI.

Thomas Hobbes (1588–1679) was an English philosopher best remembered for his book *Leviathan*, in which he established what is now known as social contract theory. Hobbes championed government, specifically the monarchy, as the supreme defense against the chaotic "state of nature."

Thomas Jefferson (1743–1826) was an American Founding Father who was the principal author of the Declaration of Independence. He later served as the third president of the United States.

Harvey J. Kaye is the Ben & Joyce Rosenberg Professor of Democracy and Justice Studies at the University of Wisconsin. He has written two books about Thomas Paine.

John Keane is a political theorist from Australia and professor of political science at the University of Sydney and at the Wissenschaftszentrum in Berlin. His current work focuses on the Asia Pacific region.

John Locke (1632–1704) was an English philosopher and is generally regarded as the father of modern liberalism. He argued that human nature was governed by reason, and some, but not all, liberties were to be given up to the state. His best-known work, *Two Treatises of Government* (1689), is considered a landmark in political thought.

King Louis XVI (1754–93) was the king of France from 1774 to 1792. After being deposed in 1792 during a period of social unrest, he was tried and eventually executed in 1793.

Jonathan Odell (1737–1818) was a poet. Loyal to the British, he suffered legal sanctions following the Revolution.

Pierre-Joseph Proudhon (1809–65) was a French politician and liberal social theorist. The founder of a branch of philosophy known as mutualism, he is also the first person to have declared himself an anarchist.

John Rawls (1921–2002) was an American philosopher and proponent of democracy. His most famous book, *A Theory of Justice*, was published in 1971 to critical acclaim.

Franklin D. Roosevelt (1882–1945) was the 32nd US president from 1933 until his death in 1945. He is the only president to have served four consecutive terms in office and was considered a master speaker.

Sophia Rosenfeld is a professor of history at the University of Virginia. She has done work in political discourse, linguistics, and analysis of revolutions.

Jean-Jacques Rousseau (1712–78) was a Genevan philosopher and member of the Enlightenment movement whose writings heavily influenced the French Revolution. Both *Discourse on the Origin of Inequality* and *On the Social Contract* are cornerstones of modern political thought.

Paul Virilio (b. 1932) is a French cultural theorist who philosophizes about the consequences of technology. One of his most important ideas is ideological contamination—the idea that technology leads to the free exchange of ideas between cultures.

Voltaire (1694–1778) is the pseudonym of François-Marie Arouet, a French Enlightenment writer who advocated, among other things, the rights of the individual and the separation of church and state. His 1756 work, *Essay on the Customs and the Spirit of the Nations*, influenced the way political thinkers looked at history.

George Washington (1732–99) was a veteran of the French and Indian War and became commander-in-chief of the Continental army on June 14, 1775, shortly after the battles of Lexington and Concord. He would later become the United States' first president in 1789.

WORKS CITED

WORKS CITED

Adams, John. *The Works of John Adams, Second President of the United States: With a Life of the Author, Notes and Illustrations.* Boston: Little, Brown, 1856. Accessed September 22, 2013. http://oll.libertyfund.org/title/2127/193637/3103690.

"Thoughts on Government." Accessed November 7, 2013. http://www.constitution.org/jadams/thoughts.htm.

Burke, Edmund. *Reflections on the Revolution in France.* Oxford: Oxford University Press, 2006.

Chalmers, James. *Plain Truth: Addressed to the Inhabitants of America, Containing, Remarks on a Late Pamphlet, Entitled Common Sense.* Charleston, SC: Nabu Press, 2014.

Conway, Moncure Daniel. *The Life of Thomas Paine: With a History of His Literary, Political and Religious Career in America, France, and England; to Which Is Added a Sketch of Paine by William Cobbett.* New York and London: G.P. Putnam and Sons, 1894.

Edelberg, Cynthia Dublin. *Jonathan Odell: The Loyalist Poet of the American Revolution.* Durham, NC: Duke University Press, 1987.

Foner, Eric. *Tom Paine and Revolutionary America.* London, New York, and Oxford: Oxford University Press, 1976.

Fukuyama, Francis. *The End of History and the Last Man.* London: Penguin, 2012.

Gould, Philip. *Writing the Rebellion: Loyalists and the Literature of Politics in British America.* New York: Oxford University Press, 2013.

Hallin, Daniel C. *The Uncensored War: The Media and Vietnam.* Berkeley: University of California Press, 1989.

Hitchens, Christopher. *Thomas Paine's Rights of Man.* New York: Grove Press, 2006.

Hobbes, Thomas. *Leviathan.* Edited by J.C.A. Gaskin. Oxford and New York: Oxford University Press, 2008.

Howarth, Stephen. *To Shining Sea: A History of the United States Navy, 1775–1998.* Norman: University of Oklahoma Press, 1991.

Jefferson, Thomas. *To Thomas Paine Philadelphia, June 19, 1792.* Accessed December 8, 2014, http://www.let.rug.nl/usa/presidents/thomas-jefferson/letters-of-thomas-jefferson/jefl99.php.

Kaye, Harvey J. *Thomas Paine and the Promise of America*. New York: Hill & Wang, 2005.

Keane, John. *Tom Paine: A Political Life*. London, New York, and Berlin: Bloomsbury, 2009.

Larkin, Edward. "Inventing an American Public: Thomas Paine, the *Pennsylvania Magazine*, and American Revolutionary Discourse." *Early American Literature* 33, no. 3 (1998): 250–76.

Locke, John. *Two Treatises of Government*. Edited by Peter Laslett. Cambridge: Cambridge University Press, 1988.

Meacham, Jon. *Thomas Jefferson: The Art of Power*. New York: Random House Trade Paperbacks; reprint edition, 2013.

Nelson, Craig. *Thomas Paine: His Life, His Time and the Birth of Modern Nations*. London: Profile Books, 2007.

Paine, Thomas. *The Age of Reason*. New York: Cosimo, 2005.

Common Sense. New York: Dover Publications Inc., 1997.

The Rights of Man. New York: Dover Publications Inc., 1999.

The Thomas Paine Reader. Edited by Michael Foot and Isaac Kramnick. London: Penguin, 1987.

The Writings of Thomas Paine. Edited by Moncure Daniel Conway. New York: G.P. Putnam's Sons, 1894. Accessed December 8, 2014, http://oll.libertyfund.org/titles/1083.

Philip, Mark. Introduction to *Rights of Man, Common Sense, and Other Political Writings*, by Thomas Paine. Oxford: Oxford University Press. 2008.

Rosenfeld, Sophia. *Common Sense: A Political History*. Cambridge, MA: Harvard University Press, 2011.

Virilio, Paul. *The Information Bomb*. Translated by Chris Turner. London: Verso, 2005.

Wraight, Christopher D. *Rousseau's* The Social Contract*: A Reader's Guide*. London and New York: Continuum, 2008.

THE MACAT LIBRARY
BY DISCIPLINE

AFRICANA STUDIES

Chinua Achebe's *An Image of Africa: Racism in Conrad's Heart of Darkness*
W. E. B. Du Bois's *The Souls of Black Folk*
Zora Neale Huston's *Characteristics of Negro Expression*
Martin Luther King Jr's *Why We Can't Wait*
Toni Morrison's *Playing in the Dark: Whiteness in the American Literary Imagination*

ANTHROPOLOGY

Arjun Appadurai's *Modernity at Large: Cultural Dimensions of Globalisation*
Philippe Ariès's *Centuries of Childhood*
Franz Boas's *Race, Language and Culture*
Kim Chan & Renée Mauborgne's *Blue Ocean Strategy*
Jared Diamond's *Guns, Germs & Steel: the Fate of Human Societies*
Jared Diamond's *Collapse: How Societies Choose to Fail or Survive*
E. E. Evans-Pritchard's *Witchcraft, Oracles and Magic Among the Azande*
James Ferguson's *The Anti-Politics Machine*
Clifford Geertz's *The Interpretation of Cultures*
David Graeber's *Debt: the First 5000 Years*
Karen Ho's *Liquidated: An Ethnography of Wall Street*
Geert Hofstede's *Culture's Consequences: Comparing Values, Behaviors, Institutes and Organizations across Nations*
Claude Lévi-Strauss's *Structural Anthropology*
Jay Macleod's *Ain't No Makin' It: Aspirations and Attainment in a Low-Income Neighborhood*
Saba Mahmood's *The Politics of Piety: The Islamic Revival and the Feminist Subject*
Marcel Mauss's *The Gift*

BUSINESS

Jean Lave & Etienne Wenger's *Situated Learning*
Theodore Levitt's *Marketing Myopia*
Burton G. Malkiel's *A Random Walk Down Wall Street*
Douglas McGregor's *The Human Side of Enterprise*
Michael Porter's *Competitive Strategy: Creating and Sustaining Superior Performance*
John Kotter's *Leading Change*
C. K. Prahalad & Gary Hamel's *The Core Competence of the Corporation*

CRIMINOLOGY

Michelle Alexander's *The New Jim Crow: Mass Incarceration in the Age of Colorblindness*
Michael R. Gottfredson & Travis Hirschi's *A General Theory of Crime*
Richard Herrnstein & Charles A. Murray's *The Bell Curve: Intelligence and Class Structure in American Life*
Elizabeth Loftus's *Eyewitness Testimony*
Jay Macleod's *Ain't No Makin' It: Aspirations and Attainment in a Low-Income Neighborhood*
Philip Zimbardo's *The Lucifer Effect*

ECONOMICS

Janet Abu-Lughod's *Before European Hegemony*
Ha-Joon Chang's *Kicking Away the Ladder*
David Brion Davis's *The Problem of Slavery in the Age of Revolution*
Milton Friedman's *The Role of Monetary Policy*
Milton Friedman's *Capitalism and Freedom*
David Graeber's *Debt: the First 5000 Years*
Friedrich Hayek's *The Road to Serfdom*
Karen Ho's *Liquidated: An Ethnography of Wall Street*

John Maynard Keynes's *The General Theory of Employment, Interest and Money*
Charles P. Kindleberger's *Manias, Panics and Crashes*
Robert Lucas's *Why Doesn't Capital Flow from Rich to Poor Countries?*
Burton G. Malkiel's *A Random Walk Down Wall Street*
Thomas Robert Malthus's *An Essay on the Principle of Population*
Karl Marx's *Capital*
Thomas Piketty's *Capital in the Twenty-First Century*
Amartya Sen's *Development as Freedom*
Adam Smith's *The Wealth of Nations*
Nassim Nicholas Taleb's *The Black Swan: The Impact of the Highly Improbable*
Amos Tversky's & Daniel Kahneman's *Judgment under Uncertainty: Heuristics and Biases*
Mahbub Ul Haq's *Reflections on Human Development*
Max Weber's *The Protestant Ethic and the Spirit of Capitalism*

FEMINISM AND GENDER STUDIES

Judith Butler's *Gender Trouble*
Simone De Beauvoir's *The Second Sex*
Michel Foucault's *History of Sexuality*
Betty Friedan's *The Feminine Mystique*
Saba Mahmood's *The Politics of Piety: The Islamic Revival and the Feminist Subject*
Joan Wallach Scott's *Gender and the Politics of History*
Mary Wollstonecraft's *A Vindication of the Rights of Woman*
Virginia Woolf's *A Room of One's Own*

GEOGRAPHY

The Brundtland Report's *Our Common Future*
Rachel Carson's *Silent Spring*
Charles Darwin's *On the Origin of Species*
James Ferguson's *The Anti-Politics Machine*
Jane Jacobs's *The Death and Life of Great American Cities*
James Lovelock's *Gaia: A New Look at Life on Earth*
Amartya Sen's *Development as Freedom*
Mathis Wackernagel & William Rees's *Our Ecological Footprint*

HISTORY

Janet Abu-Lughod's *Before European Hegemony*
Benedict Anderson's *Imagined Communities*
Bernard Bailyn's *The Ideological Origins of the American Revolution*
Hanna Batatu's *The Old Social Classes And The Revolutionary Movements Of Iraq*
Christopher Browning's *Ordinary Men: Reserve Police Batallion 101 and the Final Solution in Poland*
Edmund Burke's *Reflections on the Revolution in France*
William Cronon's *Nature's Metropolis: Chicago And The Great West*
Alfred W. Crosby's *The Columbian Exchange*
Hamid Dabashi's *Iran: A People Interrupted*
David Brion Davis's *The Problem of Slavery in the Age of Revolution*
Nathalie Zemon Davis's *The Return of Martin Guerre*
Jared Diamond's *Guns, Germs & Steel: the Fate of Human Societies*
Frank Dikotter's *Mao's Great Famine*
John W Dower's *War Without Mercy: Race And Power In The Pacific War*
W. E. B. Du Bois's *The Souls of Black Folk*
Richard J. Evans's *In Defence of History*
Lucien Febvre's *The Problem of Unbelief in the 16th Century*
Sheila Fitzpatrick's *Everyday Stalinism*

The Macat Library By Discipline

Eric Foner's *Reconstruction: America's Unfinished Revolution, 1863-1877*
Michel Foucault's *Discipline and Punish*
Michel Foucault's *History of Sexuality*
Francis Fukuyama's *The End of History and the Last Man*
John Lewis Gaddis's *We Now Know: Rethinking Cold War History*
Ernest Gellner's *Nations and Nationalism*
Eugene Genovese's *Roll, Jordan, Roll: The World the Slaves Made*
Carlo Ginzburg's *The Night Battles*
Daniel Goldhagen's *Hitler's Willing Executioners*
Jack Goldstone's *Revolution and Rebellion in the Early Modern World*
Antonio Gramsci's *The Prison Notebooks*
Alexander Hamilton, John Jay & James Madison's *The Federalist Papers*
Christopher Hill's *The World Turned Upside Down*
Carole Hillenbrand's *The Crusades: Islamic Perspectives*
Thomas Hobbes's *Leviathan*
Eric Hobsbawm's *The Age Of Revolution*
John A. Hobson's *Imperialism: A Study*
Albert Hourani's *History of the Arab Peoples*
Samuel P. Huntington's *The Clash of Civilizations and the Remaking of World Order*
C. L. R. James's *The Black Jacobins*
Tony Judt's *Postwar: A History of Europe Since 1945*
Ernst Kantorowicz's *The King's Two Bodies: A Study in Medieval Political Theology*
Paul Kennedy's *The Rise and Fall of the Great Powers*
Ian Kershaw's *The "Hitler Myth": Image and Reality in the Third Reich*
John Maynard Keynes's *The General Theory of Employment, Interest and Money*
Charles P. Kindleberger's *Manias, Panics and Crashes*
Martin Luther King Jr's *Why We Can't Wait*
Henry Kissinger's *World Order: Reflections on the Character of Nations and the Course of History*
Thomas Kuhn's *The Structure of Scientific Revolutions*
Georges Lefebvre's *The Coming of the French Revolution*
John Locke's *Two Treatises of Government*
Niccolò Machiavelli's *The Prince*
Thomas Robert Malthus's *An Essay on the Principle of Population*
Mahmood Mamdani's *Citizen and Subject: Contemporary Africa And The Legacy Of Late Colonialism*
Karl Marx's *Capital*
Stanley Milgram's *Obedience to Authority*
John Stuart Mill's *On Liberty*
Thomas Paine's *Common Sense*
Thomas Paine's *Rights of Man*
Geoffrey Parker's *Global Crisis: War, Climate Change and Catastrophe in the Seventeenth Century*
Jonathan Riley-Smith's *The First Crusade and the Idea of Crusading*
Jean-Jacques Rousseau's *The Social Contract*
Joan Wallach Scott's *Gender and the Politics of History*
Theda Skocpol's *States and Social Revolutions*
Adam Smith's *The Wealth of Nations*
Timothy Snyder's *Bloodlands: Europe Between Hitler and Stalin*
Sun Tzu's *The Art of War*
Keith Thomas's *Religion and the Decline of Magic*
Thucydides's *The History of the Peloponnesian War*
Frederick Jackson Turner's *The Significance of the Frontier in American History*
Odd Arne Westad's *The Global Cold War: Third World Interventions And The Making Of Our Times*

LITERATURE

Chinua Achebe's *An Image of Africa: Racism in Conrad's Heart of Darkness*
Roland Barthes's *Mythologies*
Homi K. Bhabha's *The Location of Culture*
Judith Butler's *Gender Trouble*
Simone De Beauvoir's *The Second Sex*
Ferdinand De Saussure's *Course in General Linguistics*
T. S. Eliot's *The Sacred Wood: Essays on Poetry and Criticism*
Zora Neale Huston's *Characteristics of Negro Expression*
Toni Morrison's *Playing in the Dark: Whiteness in the American Literary Imagination*
Edward Said's *Orientalism*
Gayatri Chakravorty Spivak's *Can the Subaltern Speak?*
Mary Wollstonecraft's *A Vindication of the Rights of Women*
Virginia Woolf's *A Room of One's Own*

PHILOSOPHY

Elizabeth Anscombe's *Modern Moral Philosophy*
Hannah Arendt's *The Human Condition*
Aristotle's *Metaphysics*
Aristotle's *Nicomachean Ethics*
Edmund Gettier's *Is Justified True Belief Knowledge?*
Georg Wilhelm Friedrich Hegel's *Phenomenology of Spirit*
David Hume's *Dialogues Concerning Natural Religion*
David Hume's *The Enquiry for Human Understanding*
Immanuel Kant's *Religion within the Boundaries of Mere Reason*
Immanuel Kant's *Critique of Pure Reason*
Søren Kierkegaard's *The Sickness Unto Death*
Søren Kierkegaard's *Fear and Trembling*
C. S. Lewis's *The Abolition of Man*
Alasdair MacIntyre's *After Virtue*
Marcus Aurelius's *Meditations*
Friedrich Nietzsche's *On the Genealogy of Morality*
Friedrich Nietzsche's *Beyond Good and Evil*
Plato's *Republic*
Plato's *Symposium*
Jean-Jacques Rousseau's *The Social Contract*
Gilbert Ryle's *The Concept of Mind*
Baruch Spinoza's *Ethics*
Sun Tzu's *The Art of War*
Ludwig Wittgenstein's *Philosophical Investigations*

POLITICS

Benedict Anderson's *Imagined Communities*
Aristotle's *Politics*
Bernard Bailyn's *The Ideological Origins of the American Revolution*
Edmund Burke's *Reflections on the Revolution in France*
John C. Calhoun's *A Disquisition on Government*
Ha-Joon Chang's *Kicking Away the Ladder*
Hamid Dabashi's *Iran: A People Interrupted*
Hamid Dabashi's *Theology of Discontent: The Ideological Foundation of the Islamic Revolution in Iran*
Robert Dahl's *Democracy and its Critics*
Robert Dahl's *Who Governs?*
David Brion Davis's *The Problem of Slavery in the Age of Revolution*

Alexis De Tocqueville's *Democracy in America*
James Ferguson's *The Anti-Politics Machine*
Frank Dikotter's *Mao's Great Famine*
Sheila Fitzpatrick's *Everyday Stalinism*
Eric Foner's *Reconstruction: America's Unfinished Revolution, 1863-1877*
Milton Friedman's *Capitalism and Freedom*
Francis Fukuyama's *The End of History and the Last Man*
John Lewis Gaddis's *We Now Know: Rethinking Cold War History*
Ernest Gellner's *Nations and Nationalism*
David Graeber's *Debt: the First 5000 Years*
Antonio Gramsci's *The Prison Notebooks*
Alexander Hamilton, John Jay & James Madison's *The Federalist Papers*
Friedrich Hayek's *The Road to Serfdom*
Christopher Hill's *The World Turned Upside Down*
Thomas Hobbes's *Leviathan*
John A. Hobson's *Imperialism: A Study*
Samuel P. Huntington's *The Clash of Civilizations and the Remaking of World Order*
Tony Judt's *Postwar: A History of Europe Since 1945*
David C. Kang's *China Rising: Peace, Power and Order in East Asia*
Paul Kennedy's *The Rise and Fall of Great Powers*
Robert Keohane's *After Hegemony*
Martin Luther King Jr.'s *Why We Can't Wait*
Henry Kissinger's *World Order: Reflections on the Character of Nations and the Course of History*
John Locke's *Two Treatises of Government*
Niccolò Machiavelli's *The Prince*
Thomas Robert Malthus's *An Essay on the Principle of Population*
Mahmood Mamdani's *Citizen and Subject: Contemporary Africa And The Legacy Of Late Colonialism*
Karl Marx's *Capital*
John Stuart Mill's *On Liberty*
John Stuart Mill's *Utilitarianism*
Hans Morgenthau's *Politics Among Nations*
Thomas Paine's *Common Sense*
Thomas Paine's *Rights of Man*
Thomas Piketty's *Capital in the Twenty-First Century*
Robert D. Putman's *Bowling Alone*
John Rawls's *Theory of Justice*
Jean-Jacques Rousseau's *The Social Contract*
Theda Skocpol's *States and Social Revolutions*
Adam Smith's *The Wealth of Nations*
Sun Tzu's *The Art of War*
Henry David Thoreau's *Civil Disobedience*
Thucydides's *The History of the Peloponnesian War*
Kenneth Waltz's *Theory of International Politics*
Max Weber's *Politics as a Vocation*
Odd Arne Westad's *The Global Cold War: Third World Interventions And The Making Of Our Times*

POSTCOLONIAL STUDIES

Roland Barthes's *Mythologies*
Frantz Fanon's *Black Skin, White Masks*
Homi K. Bhabha's *The Location of Culture*
Gustavo Gutiérrez's *A Theology of Liberation*
Edward Said's *Orientalism*
Gayatri Chakravorty Spivak's *Can the Subaltern Speak?*

PSYCHOLOGY

Gordon Allport's *The Nature of Prejudice*
Alan Baddeley & Graham Hitch's *Aggression: A Social Learning Analysis*
Albert Bandura's *Aggression: A Social Learning Analysis*
Leon Festinger's *A Theory of Cognitive Dissonance*
Sigmund Freud's *The Interpretation of Dreams*
Betty Friedan's *The Feminine Mystique*
Michael R. Gottfredson & Travis Hirschi's *A General Theory of Crime*
Eric Hoffer's *The True Believer: Thoughts on the Nature of Mass Movements*
William James's *Principles of Psychology*
Elizabeth Loftus's *Eyewitness Testimony*
A. H. Maslow's *A Theory of Human Motivation*
Stanley Milgram's *Obedience to Authority*
Steven Pinker's *The Better Angels of Our Nature*
Oliver Sacks's *The Man Who Mistook His Wife For a Hat*
Richard Thaler & Cass Sunstein's *Nudge: Improving Decisions About Health, Wealth and Happiness*
Amos Tversky's *Judgment under Uncertainty: Heuristics and Biases*
Philip Zimbardo's *The Lucifer Effect*

SCIENCE

Rachel Carson's *Silent Spring*
William Cronon's *Nature's Metropolis: Chicago And The Great West*
Alfred W. Crosby's *The Columbian Exchange*
Charles Darwin's *On the Origin of Species*
Richard Dawkin's *The Selfish Gene*
Thomas Kuhn's *The Structure of Scientific Revolutions*
Geoffrey Parker's *Global Crisis: War, Climate Change and Catastrophe in the Seventeenth Century*
Mathis Wackernagel & William Rees's *Our Ecological Footprint*

SOCIOLOGY

Michelle Alexander's *The New Jim Crow: Mass Incarceration in the Age of Colorblindness*
Gordon Allport's *The Nature of Prejudice*
Albert Bandura's *Aggression: A Social Learning Analysis*
Hanna Batatu's *The Old Social Classes And The Revolutionary Movements Of Iraq*
Ha-Joon Chang's *Kicking Away the Ladder*
W. E. B. Du Bois's *The Souls of Black Folk*
Émile Durkheim's *On Suicide*
Frantz Fanon's *Black Skin, White Masks*
Frantz Fanon's *The Wretched of the Earth*
Eric Foner's *Reconstruction: America's Unfinished Revolution, 1863-1877*
Eugene Genovese's *Roll, Jordan, Roll: The World the Slaves Made*
Jack Goldstone's *Revolution and Rebellion in the Early Modern World*
Antonio Gramsci's *The Prison Notebooks*
Richard Herrnstein & Charles A Murray's *The Bell Curve: Intelligence and Class Structure in American Life*
Eric Hoffer's *The True Believer: Thoughts on the Nature of Mass Movements*
Jane Jacobs's *The Death and Life of Great American Cities*
Robert Lucas's *Why Doesn't Capital Flow from Rich to Poor Countries?*
Jay Macleod's *Ain't No Makin' It: Aspirations and Attainment in a Low Income Neighborhood*
Elaine May's *Homeward Bound: American Families in the Cold War Era*
Douglas McGregor's *The Human Side of Enterprise*
C. Wright Mills's *The Sociological Imagination*

Thomas Piketty's *Capital in the Twenty-First Century*
Robert D. Putman's *Bowling Alone*
David Riesman's *The Lonely Crowd: A Study of the Changing American Character*
Edward Said's *Orientalism*
Joan Wallach Scott's *Gender and the Politics of History*
Theda Skocpol's *States and Social Revolutions*
Max Weber's *The Protestant Ethic and the Spirit of Capitalism*

THEOLOGY

Augustine's *Confessions*
Benedict's *Rule of St Benedict*
Gustavo Gutiérrez's *A Theology of Liberation*
Carole Hillenbrand's *The Crusades: Islamic Perspectives*
David Hume's *Dialogues Concerning Natural Religion*
Immanuel Kant's *Religion within the Boundaries of Mere Reason*
Ernst Kantorowicz's *The King's Two Bodies: A Study in Medieval Political Theology*
Søren Kierkegaard's *The Sickness Unto Death*
C. S. Lewis's *The Abolition of Man*
Saba Mahmood's *The Politics of Piety: The Islamic Revival and the Feminist Subject*
Baruch Spinoza's *Ethics*
Keith Thomas's *Religion and the Decline of Magic*

COMING SOON

Chris Argyris's *The Individual and the Organisation*
Seyla Benhabib's *The Rights of Others*
Walter Benjamin's *The Work Of Art in the Age of Mechanical Reproduction*
John Berger's *Ways of Seeing*
Pierre Bourdieu's *Outline of a Theory of Practice*
Mary Douglas's *Purity and Danger*
Roland Dworkin's *Taking Rights Seriously*
James G. March's *Exploration and Exploitation in Organisational Learning*
Ikujiro Nonaka's *A Dynamic Theory of Organizational Knowledge Creation*
Griselda Pollock's *Vision and Difference*
Amartya Sen's *Inequality Re-Examined*
Susan Sontag's *On Photography*
Yasser Tabbaa's *The Transformation of Islamic Art*
Ludwig von Mises's *Theory of Money and Credit*

Macat Disciplines

Access the greatest ideas and thinkers across entire disciplines, including

FEMINISM, GENDER AND QUEER STUDIES

Simone De Beauvoir's
The Second Sex

Michel Foucault's
History of Sexuality

Betty Friedan's
The Feminine Mystique

Saba Mahmood's
*The Politics of Piety:
The Islamic Revival and
the Feminist Subject*

Joan Wallach Scott's
*Gender and the
Politics of History*

Mary Wollstonecraft's
*A Vindication of the
Rights of Woman*

Virginia Woolf's
A Room of One's Own

Judith Butler's
Gender Trouble

Macat analyses are available from all good bookshops and libraries.

Access hundreds of analyses through one, multimedia tool.
Join free for one month **library.macat.com**

Macat Disciplines

Access the greatest ideas and thinkers across entire disciplines, including

INEQUALITY

Ha-Joon Chang's, *Kicking Away the Ladder*

David Graeber's, *Debt: The First 5000 Years*

Robert E. Lucas's, *Why Doesn't Capital Flow from Rich To Poor Countries?*

Thomas Piketty's, *Capital in the Twenty-First Century*

Amartya Sen's, *Inequality Re-Examined*

Mahbub Ul Haq's, *Reflections on Human Development*

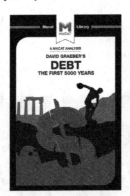

Macat analyses are available from all good bookshops and libraries

Access hundreds of analyses through one, multimedia tool.

Join free for one month **library.macat.com**

Macat Disciplines

Access the greatest ideas and thinkers across entire disciplines, including

CRIMINOLOGY

Michelle Alexander's
*The New Jim Crow:
Mass Incarceration in the
Age of Colorblindness*

**Michael R. Gottfredson
& Travis Hirschi's**
A General Theory of Crime

Elizabeth Loftus's
Eyewitness Testimony

**Richard Herrnstein
& Charles A. Murray's**
*The Bell Curve: Intelligence and
Class Structure in American Life*

Jay Macleod's
*Ain't No Makin' It:
Aspirations and Attainment in a
Low-Income Neighborhood*

Philip Zimbardo's
The Lucifer Effect

Macat Disciplines

Access the greatest ideas and thinkers across entire disciplines, including

Postcolonial Studies

Roland Barthes's *Mythologies*
Frantz Fanon's *Black Skin, White Masks*
Homi K. Bhabha's *The Location of Culture*
Gustavo Gutiérrez's *A Theology of Liberation*
Edward Said's *Orientalism*
Gayatri Chakravorty Spivak's *Can the Subaltern Speak?*

Macat Disciplines

*Access the greatest ideas and thinkers
across entire disciplines, including*

GLOBALIZATION

Arjun Appadurai's, *Modernity at Large:
Cultural Dimensions of Globalisation*

James Ferguson's, *The Anti-Politics Machine*

Geert Hofstede's, *Culture's Consequences*

Amartya Sen's, *Development as Freedom*

Macat Pairs

Analyse historical and modern issues from opposite sides of an argument. Pairs include:

HOW TO RUN AN ECONOMY

John Maynard Keynes's
The General Theory OF Employment, Interest and Money

Classical economics suggests that market economies are self-correcting in times of recession or depression, and tend toward full employment and output. But English economist John Maynard Keynes disagrees.

In his ground-breaking 1936 study *The General Theory*, Keynes argues that traditional economics has misunderstood the causes of unemployment. Employment is not determined by the price of labor; it is directly linked to demand. Keynes believes market economies are by nature unstable, and so require government intervention. Spurred on by the social catastrophe of the Great Depression of the 1930s, he sets out to revolutionize the way the world thinks

Milton Friedman's
The Role of Monetary Policy

Friedman's 1968 paper changed the course of economic theory. In just 17 pages, he demolished existing theory and outlined an effective alternate monetary policy designed to secure 'high employment stable prices and rapid growth.'

Friedman demonstrated that monetary policy plays a vital role in broader economic stability and argued that economists got their monetary policy wrong in the 1950s and 1960s by misunderstanding the relationship between inflation and unemployment. Previous generations of economists had believed that governments could permanently decrease unemployment by permitting inflation—and vice vers Friedman's most original contribution was to show th this supposed trade-off is an illusion that only works the short term.

Macat Disciplines

Access the greatest ideas and thinkers across entire disciplines, including

TOTALITARIANISM

Sheila Fitzpatrick's, *Everyday Stalinism*
Ian Kershaw's, *The "Hitler Myth"*
Timothy Snyder's, *Bloodlands*

Macat Pairs

Analyse historical and modern issues from opposite sides of an argument. Pairs include:

RACE AND IDENTITY

Zora Neale Hurston's
Characteristics of Negro Expression

Using material collected on anthropological expeditions to the South, Zora Neale Hurston explains how expression in African American culture in the early twentieth century departs from the art of white America. At the time, African American art was often criticized for copying white culture. For Hurston, this criticism misunderstood how art works. European tradition views art as something fixed. But Hurston describes a creative process that is alive, ever-changing, and largely improvisational. She maintains that African American art works through a process called 'mimicry'—where an imitated object or verbal pattern, for example, is reshaped and altered until it becomes something new, novel—and worthy of attention.

Frantz Fanon's
Black Skin, White Masks

Black Skin, White Masks offers a radical analysis of the psychological effects of colonization on the colonized.

Fanon witnessed the effects of colonization first hand both in his birthplace, Martinique, and again later in life when he worked as a psychiatrist in another French colony, Algeria. His text is uncompromising in form and argument. He dissects the dehumanizing effects of colonialism, arguing that it destroys the native sense of identity, forcing people to adapt to an alien set of values—including a core belief that they are inferior. This results in deep psychological trauma.

Fanon's work played a pivotal role in the civil rights movements of the 1960s.

Macat Pairs

Analyse historical and modern issues from opposite sides of an argument. Pairs include:

INTERNATIONAL RELATIONS IN THE 21ST CENTURY

Samuel P. Huntington's
The Clash of Civilisations

In his highly influential 1996 book, Huntington offers a vision of a post-Cold War world in which conflict takes place not between competing ideologies but between cultures. The worst clash, he argues, will be between the Islamic world and the West: the West's arrogance and belief that its culture is a "gift" to the world will come into conflict with Islam's obstinacy and concern that its culture is under attack from a morally decadent "other."

Clash inspired much debate between different political schools of thought. But its greatest impact came in helping define American foreign policy in the wake of the 2001 terrorist attacks in New York and Washington.

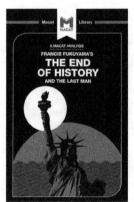

Francis Fukuyama's
The End of History and the Last Man

Published in 1992, *The End of History and the Last Man* argues that capitalist democracy is the final destination for all societies. Fukuyama believed democracy triumphed during the Cold War because it lacks the "fundamental contradictions" inherent in communism and satisfies our yearning for freedom and equality. Democracy therefore marks the endpoint in the evolution of ideology, and so the "end of history." There will still be "events," but no fundamental change in ideology.

Macat Disciplines

Access the greatest ideas and thinkers across entire disciplines, including

MAN AND THE ENVIRONMENT

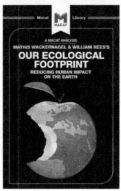

The Brundtland Report's, *Our Common Future*
Rachel Carson's, *Silent Spring*
James Lovelock's, *Gaia: A New Look at Life on Earth*
Mathis Wackernagel & William Rees's, *Our Ecological Footprint*

Macat analyses are available from all good bookshops and libraries.

Access hundreds of analyses through one, multimedia tool.
Join free for one month **library.macat.com**

Printed in the United States
by Baker & Taylor Publisher Services